# CINQUE TERRE

# TERRE

## and Riviera di Levante

### a countryside guide

Georg Henke

SUNFLOWER BOOKS

Copyright © 2014
Sunflower Books™
PO Box 36160
London SW7 3WS, UK
www.sunflowerbooks.co.uk

ISBN 978-1-85691-452-9

*Portovenere: San Pietro*

# Important note to the reader

We have tried to ensure that the descriptions and maps in this book
are error-free at press date. It will be very helpful for us to receive
your comments (sent in care of the publishers, please) for the
updating of future editions.

    We also rely on those who use this book — especially walkers —
to take along a good supply of common sense when they explore.
Conditions can change fairly rapidly on this part of the Italian Riviera,
and *storm damage or bulldozing may make a route unsafe at any time*.
If the route is not as we outline it here, and your way ahead is not
secure, return to the point of departure. *Never attempt to complete a
tour or walk under hazardous conditions!* Please read carefully the
notes on pages 11 to 14, as well as the introductory comments at the
beginning of each walk (regarding equipment, grade, distances and
time, etc). Explore *safely*, while at the same time respecting the beauty
of the countryside.

*Cover photograph: Portovenere's harbour*
*Title page: small medieval relief in the old town of Tellaro*

Photographs: Georg Henke
Maps: Nick Hill for Sunflower Books; area map data © OpenStreet
    Map
A CIP catalogue record for this book is available from the British
    Library.
Printed and bound in England: Short Run Press

# Contents

# Preface

The Mediterranean coast between Nizza (Nice) and La Spezia, the 'Riviera', was the birthplace of modern tourism in the early 1800s. The beauty of the landscape, the unspoilt and colourful old towns by the sea, the mild climate and the abundant subtropical vegetation attracted the upper classes who could afford the luxury of a leisurely stay in the warmth of the south. They came from England, Russia and Germany, fleeing the freezing north for the mild coasts of Nice, San Remo, Portofino or Rapallo. These wealthy people spent their days gambling in the casinos; hiking along stony mule trails or swimming in salt water was definitely *not* what a break in the Med was all about!

Today the Riviera's many foreign visitors no longer come in winter but mainly to enjoy a summer beach holiday. But over the last 30 years the eastern part of

*Descent towards Portovenere (Walk 5)*

the area, the Riviera di Levante between Genoa and La Spezia, has also become a much-loved hiking area — perhaps the most popular in all Italy apart from the Alps. And the 'Cinque Terre', the steep coast south of Levanto cradling the five villages of Monterosso, Vernazza, Corniglia, Manarola and Riomaggiore, is the best loved of all, attracting great numbers of hikers from as far afield as the States, Canada, Australia, New Zealand, Japan and China.

There are good reasons for this meteoric rise from a remote area of simple vine-growers and fishermen to a hot spot of modern tourism featuring in so many articles on Italy: the colourful houses of the five villages, nestled against steep terraced slopes above the blue sea and still connected by old cobbled mule trails, take the visitor back to the times when the Italian coast was still unspoilt by modern civilisation. That's why this small area has been designated as an Italian national park and a UNESCO world heritage site.

The popularity of the Cinque Terre has its price. It's still as picturesque as ever, but one only experiences the 'away from it all' feeling now in winter, when the tourists are gone. Still, it *is* easy to escape the masses, even in high season. The Riviera di Levante is not only the Cinque Terre! There are many other places where

steep mountains border the sea, painting a varied landscape of bays and promontories. For instance, around the Gulf of La Spezia, in the 'little Cinque Terre' to the north of Levanto, and across the Portofino Peninsula you'll find attractive trails high on the slopes above the coast, and they are much less crowded but similar in scenery to those in the Cinque Terre itself.

Further inland, the sparsely inhabited Apennines, which cross the whole Italian Peninsula from Liguria to Calabria, offer up a totally different landscape. This is a remote area of high pastures, mixed forests and barren ridges; the mild coast with its bays and beaches surrounded by olive and pine tree-covered hills seems very far away from here, although it's only some 30 kilometres between the sea and the mountains. This more Nordic-looking area has plenty of hiking trails, but it doesn't satisfy the expectations of visitors seeking the charm of the Mediterranean. That's why foreign visitors tend to ignore this hinterland — and why nearly all the walks in this book keep to the coast. (But if you want to get an impression of these uplands, then *do* try Walk 19 or Walk 26.)

Sunflower's *Landscapes* guides normally feature car touring and picnicking sections. But the Riviera di Levante, a small stretch of land trapped between the sea

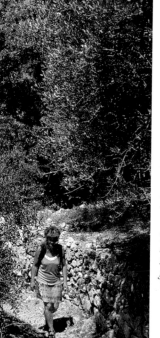

and the mountains, just does not lend itself to touring by car. Moreover, the towns and villages are so tightly packed that parking is a major problem and almost invariably very expensive — especially in the Cinque Terre. Above all, there is no need to have a car: all the walks in this book can be reached by public transport — whether train, bus or boat.

*The walk descriptions and accompanying maps will give you some ideas about where to find good picnic spots. This is Walk 11 above Tellaro.*

# Getting there and getting about

Northwestern Italy is well served by two international airports: Milan's Malpensa in Lombardy and Pisa's Galileo Galilei in Tuscany, whereas there are very few arrivals from abroad at Liguria's main airport, Cristofero Colombo in Genoa. But there *are* daily direct flights from London Gatwick (BA) and Stanstead (Ryanair) to **Genoa**. From the airport there's a shuttle bus *(volabus)* every 30 to 45 minutes to the main railway stations of Piazza Principe and Brignole, crossing the city centre. From Piazza Principe station it takes about 1h10min by intercity train or 1h30min by regional train to Monterosso in the Cinque Terre.

From **Pisa** the Cinque Terre can easily be reached by train via La Spezia. All year round there are direct flights to Pisa from London Heathrow (BA), Gatwick (Easyjet and Ryanair), Stanstead (Ryanair) and Bristol (Easyjet). In summer there is also a non-stop Delta flight four times a week from New York's JFK. From Pisa's airport frequent buses make the 10-minute run to the central railway station from 6 am till midnight. It takes about an hour by fast train to La Spezia, where you have to change to a local train serving the five villages.

**Milan's** large Malpensa airport receives the widest range of non-stop air services from the UK. There are also direct flights from several places in the States. Once there, a bus leaves the airport for the inner city and the central railway station (Milano Centrale) every 20 minutes from 5 am till midnight. Then it's about 1h40min to Genoa and the good west coast main line travels on towards La Spezia, frequently serving all the coastal towns and villages featuring in this book.

There are different sorts of trains: fast Frecciarossa heading for Rome, slightly slower intercity trains from Milano Centrale to Pisa/Livorno which stop more frequently, regional trains *(treno regionale)* which stop at all but the very small stations, and snail's-pace local trains *(treno locale)* which stop nearly everywhere. In all,

8

*Monterosso Beach*

about 15 faster Frecciarossa or intercity trains run from Milan to Pisa and Rome via Genoa and La Spezia, most of which stop at Rapallo and Chiavari en route. About six intercity trains also stop at Santa Margherita Ligure, Sestri Levante, Levanto and Monterosso. Monterosso is the only station of the Cinque Terre served by fast trains (three hours from Milan).

For those coming from Asia or Australia, **Rome's** Fiumincino Airport has the widest choice of flights. Then the fast Leonardo Express runs non-stop from the airport to the central railway station (Roma Central), which has about eight trains a day to Pisa, La Spezia and Genoa. It takes about 3h45min from Rome up to La Spezia.

There is about one local or regional train per hour along the coastal main line, and more between Sestri Levante and Genoa. From May to October there are additional connections from Levanto to La Spezia serving the villages of the Cinque Terre. The fares on local trains are low; they are more costly on the Frecciarossa and intercity trains, but still reasonable (except for very short distances). For Frecciarossa and intercity trains you need to reserve seats in advance (normally one can do this in the stations and at short notice). Timetables and pre-booking from abroad are offered on www.trenitalia.com.

Public buses are only of local importance, especially between Sestri Levante and La Spezia, where only a few short lines connect the inland villages to the railway stations. There are more frequent buses to the north of Sestri Levante, heading towards Genoa and around La Spezia Bay. Buses are as cheap as local trains but often much slower.

More details on public transport, timetables and rail lines are given overleaf, in the introductory notes for each area and at the start of the walks themselves.

## Public transport

All the walks in this book can be reached by public transport. Most of them require the use of trains, buses or boats, as they are linear. Details of bus/train/boat timetables are given for each walk (valid at the time of writing).

In Italy timings change at least twice a year — in mid-June when the summer timetable *(orario estivo)* begins, and in mid-September with the start of the winter timetable *(orario invernale)*. But timetables can change at short notice at any time, so the times given in the book can only be taken as an *approximation* of the public transport situation at a certain place.

To check up-to-date **bus timetables** on the web:
— for all lines from Levanto to Genoa go to **www.atpesercizio.it** *('percorsi e orari')*
— for all lines from Levanto to La Spezia/Lerici go to **www.atcesercicio.it** *('Visualizza il Libretto orario')*

*Timetable translation hints:*
*Feriale:* runs on workdays (Mon-Sat)
*Feriale escl. Sabato* or *Lun-Ven:* runs on workdays except Saturdays
*Festivo:* runs only on Sundays and public holidays

Before boarding a bus, get your ticket *(biglietto)* at small shops with a T-sign *(tabacchi)*, at a bar or newspaper kiosk. Validate it by stamping it in the yellow box when boarding the vehicle. While you can often buy tickets from the bus drivers, it normally costs twice as much.

Many walks in the book require a short **train** ride. Validate each train ticket in one of the yellow or green automats at the railway station before boarding. Otherwise you may have to pay about 50 euros penalty for ticketless riding! Tickets for short rides can also be bought at automats, bars, kiosks and Cinque Terre National Park offices (at all railway stations from Levanto to La Spezia).

You can tell if you're facing in the right direction on the train platforms by looking at the signs to 'La Spezia' (southbound trains) and 'Genova' (northbound). In the Cinque Terre you may have to get off the train in a tunnel because the stations are so small! It is strictly forbidden to walk across the tracks; always use the underground passage *(sottopassaggio)*. For online train timetables go to **www. trenitalia.com**.

# ✿ Walking

Italians don't hike! Well, that's what everyone says anyway. But you'll see just how wrong they are when you visit the Cinque Terre on a sunny weekend — when there are not only walkers from abroad, but plenty of residents of Genoa, Milan and Bologna on these busy coastal trails. Until a few decades ago walking as a leisure activity was largely unknown in Italy outside the nature reserves in the Alps. But gradually a change of attitude has made itself felt throughout the country. Local residents have started to explore the scenic beauty of their native land, and in many places hiking routes have been waymarked and signposted. Today the Cinque Terre — and, to a lesser degree, the Portofino Peninsula — are among the most popular walking destinations in all Italy. So when you follow these well-worn trails there will almost always be other hikers about. By contrast, the trails in the other areas featured in this book are still quite empty.

## Maps and waymarks

Nowadays various publishers produce **walking maps** *(Carta dei Sentieri)* at a scale of 1:25,000 covering the whole Riviera di Levante. Unfortunately these maps are only reliable when it comes to topography. In most cases the routes shown — whether paths, trails, tracks or even the smaller tarmac roads — are not fully up-to-date. Sometimes the bold red lines shown on the maps, which should indicate waymarked, well-established routes, turn out to be thickly overgrown or not to exist at all. Conversely, the maps may omit obvious trails.

The most appropriate hiking map for each of the walks in this book is mentioned in the introductory text. But the maps in this book, together with the walking notes, should be sufficient for your route-finding.

Nearly all walking trails on the Riviera di Levante are **waymarked** nowadays, and there are often sign-posts at intersections and forks. In the southern part of the area, to the south of Deiva Marina, the waymarks are nearly always double white stripes on a red ground, sometimes with the appropriate route number in black. In the northern part of the region waymarking usually

11

consists of different red symbols — like squares, circles, dots, rhombi, crosses, etc. The waymarking is not always 100% reliable: sometimes the marks fade out in the middle of the walk, suddenly to reappear later, or the colouring/style of waymarking may change en route for no obvious reason.

Because the mapping and waymarking are not always reliable, I have tried to make my descriptions of the walks so comprehensive that you should have no trouble finding your way *without* waymarks. Bear in mind, too, that some of my walks follow only *part of* a waymarked route, so *always refer to the description!* Waymarks which where on the ground at the time of writing are mentioned, but I certainly cannot guarantee that they will still be there in two or three years' time.

## When to walk

The Italian Riviera has a very mild climate, with temperatures rarely falling below zero. Except for the high Apennines, walking is possible all year round. **Spring** (April to mid-June) is the best season: temperatures are pleasant, many wild plants are in bloom, and often a clear blue sky arches above the sea and the mountains. **Autumn** (mid-September to the end of October) can be just as good as far as weather goes. But in both spring and autumn be prepared for rain every now and then, especially from April to mid-May and in October. In general any wet weather will not last very long. During high summer it's often very hot, and the only way to enjoy a walk is to start at sunrise and get back to base by noon at the latest.

It's also pleasant to walk from **November to March**, at least if you keep close to the coast, which sees less rainfall and higher temperatures than the mountains. Of course the weather will be unpredictable — it may rain for days on end or be fairly warm and sunny!

In the higher mountains of the **Apennines**, especially in the Aveto Nature Park, conditions are of course a bit different. You can even hike here in high summer, while in winter the ground — at a height of over 1000m — is often covered with snow.

## Equipment

No special equipment is needed for any walk in this book, but good **walking boots** with sturdy soles and good ankle protection are highly recommended, as

*Terrazzamento, the system of drystone sustaining walls described on page 16. This is Walk 4 near Corniglia.*

many routes cross stony and sometimes sloping terrain. And just because the coastal trails of the Cinque Terre are so popular doesn't mean they are easy strolls! In the high Apennines you should always have a **waterproof and extra clothing** with you, as the weather is unpredictable and may change suddenly.

From May to October always take **sun protection** (hat, cream, glasses); many routes have long sections in full sun. Because many walks offer no chance for refreshment en route, take enough **food** and — even more important — plenty of **drinking water** (at least 1.5 litres for a whole day, 2.5 litres in summer) in a refillable container. Some walks pass springs and fountains with drinking water *(acqua potabile)*. On warm days, when there are long ascents, you will need *a lot* of water. Several walks visit or end near beaches; don't forget to take **swimwear!**

All year round you should take a small **first aid kit**, a knife, a whistle, extra socks and shoelaces and warm clothing. **Long trousers** and a **shirt with long sleeves** protect against sunburn and thorny plants. **Walking sticks** are very useful, as there are some steep descents en route; they lessen the wear on your ankles and knees and give support on tricky descents, when fords have to be crossed, and when obstacles, undergrowth or unfriendly dogs block the route.

## A country code for walkers

• Because of the danger of forest fires, **open fires** should only be lit at specially provided barbecue places; in dry weather, it is best to light no fires at all.
• If at all possible **avoid straying from the paths**. Taking short cuts across fields will damage the vegetation and will lead to the erosion of the main path.
• **Ensure that gates are always closed**, even if there are no animals in sight.

- **Do not pick wild flowers** or cultivated plants and do not help yourself to fruit from gardens or vineyards. Small losses add up and will annoy farmers.
- **Take all rubbish away with you**.
- **Do not frighten animals** or provoke watchdogs.
- **Be considerate and polite** in your behaviour towards local people. Respect private property and walk quickly past inhabited houses and farms.
- Autumn is the **hunting season**. Take care walking in open country outside nature reserves (where hunting is forbidden). Do not leave the route, and if hunters are nearby draw attention to yourself by shouting loudly.

## Walk descriptions, grading

The walks in this book range from **simple rambles** on well-worn footpaths and paved walkways to **long hikes** on steep and narrow mountain trails. (Although fairly demanding, the latter do not require mountaineering skills, although Walks 21 and 25 do call for a little clambering over rocks.)

The walks are **graded** for walkers with average fitness. A walking speed of 4km/h on flat terrain and an ascent of 350m per hour are taken as a basis. Times shown are neat walking times. When planning your walk, be sure to increase given times by *at least* a third, to allow for rest breaks, taking pictures and sightseeing.

In Italy walking is normally a combination of opulent picnicking and pretty demanding hiking. Even on some of the main waymarked routes you may come upon short 'delicate' sections (sloping rocks, steep stony descents, narrow exposed paths beside precipices and the like). While none of these is an insurmountable obstacle to the average hiker, those lacking a head for heights or who are less sure-footed and agile on stony sloping ground should read the full description of the walk in advance, to be prepared for possible difficulties.

Below is a key to the symbols on the walking maps:

| | | | | | |
|---|---|---|---|---|---|
| ≡E41≡ | motorway | ▲ ■ ● | types of waymarks | † | cross.tabernacle |
| | main road | 400 | height in metres | + | cemetery |
| | secondary road | 🚌 | bus stop | ■ | fort.castle |
| | minor road | 🚆 | railway station | | watchtower |
| | track | 🚋 | rack railway station | ⊼ | picnic tables |
| - - - - | path, trail | ⛴ | ferry quay | | best views |
| →2  →2 | main/alternative walk with official route number | ⛟ | funicular | λ | transmitter mast |
| | | ⛏ | walkers' signpost | ∩ | cave |
| 5 | other walk described in this book, with its number | ◆▶ | spring | ☼ | mill |
| | | ⛪ | church.chapel | | watchtower |

# Cinque Terre

## a walkers' paradise

*Riomaggiore*

**P**robably nowhere else in Italy will you find a more scenic stretch of uncontaminated rugged coast as in the Cinque Terre to the north of La Spezia. Even today the 'five lands' — the villages of Monterosso, Vernazza, Corniglia, Manarola and Riomaggiore — present an unspoilt image from the Mediterranean picture book. Nestled among steep slopes and cliffs above the crystal-blue sea, with their colourful houses, old churches and narrow alleyways, they seem to have been lost in time. Due to the steep and harsh terrain, the 20-kilometre-long shoreline between Levanto and Portovenere was for centuries only accessible by land on small cobbled mule trails. Thanks to their relative remoteness, they are still beautiful today.

The Cinque Terre has always been a region of vineyards. Because of the steep terrain the grapes can only be cultivated on small terraces. These typical little vineyards have contributed to the creation of *terrazzamento,* a system of drystone retaining walls. There are several thousand kilometres of these walls, which prevent the precious soil from being washed down into the sea.

Today the beauty of the area is no longer an insiders' tip. From April to October masses of tourists come here, many of them from as far afield as New Zealand, China or Canada. Most of them are attracted by the superb hiking along the panoramic paths high above the sea. There's no tarmac road along the coast. But an extensive network of old, often beautifully cobbled trails stretches from coastal village to coastal village and up to the inland hamlets, houses and forests.

Luckily the tourist boom has left the picturesque appearance of the villages and surroundings untouched. But it has brought about an important social change: tourism, not viniculture, is now the main source of income. And this of course also affects the landscape. With wine-growing in decline, many of the vineyards are now abandoned — just broken walls and terraces overgrown with macchia and oak. Sooner or later the typical landscape of the *terrazzamento* will disappear. The creation of the **Cinque Terre National Park** in 1997 is an effort to stop this process of decline. For this reason you have to pay an entrance fee for the region's most popular coastal hike: from Monterosso to Riomaggiore. The fees are used to finance the expensive maintenance work on the terraces, walls and old paths. **There are Park information offices at all railway stations from Levanto to La Spezia**; they can give you details of rooms to let, railway timetables, and up-to-date path conditions; they also sell walking maps.

All five villages have their own character and flavour. **Monterosso al Mare** is a little less picturesque, but bigger and livelier than the other four, more a little town than a village. It has the widest range of hotels, restaurants and wine bars *(enotece)*. It also offers the best swimming at its beautiful long sandy beach (shown on page 9). Monterosso is made up of two parts, the historic old town centre around PIAZZA MATTEOTTI and PIAZZA GARIBALDI, with some colourful narrow lanes, and the more modern FEGINA one kilometre to the west, by the railway station. In the old town the medieval church of SAN GIOVANNI BATTISTA, with its distinct black stripes and marble rose window is worth seeing. The 16th-century CAPUCHIN MONASTERY on top of the hill above the old centre has some fine paintings.

The multicoloured cube-like houses of **Vernazza** are nestled around a small harbour overlooked by a 14th-century church. Many guidebook covers feature photographs of Vernazza's MEDIEVAL WATCHTOWER on the steep rocky promontory pointing out to sea. Vernazza is unquestionably the most picturesque of the five villages. But it's also the most touristic: from April to October VIA ROMA in the centre, with its bars and little shops, is crowded with foreign visitors walking from the railway station down to the scenic harbour. There, by the water, the bell tower of the 1318 parish church of SANTA MARGHERITA rises above the cosy piazza with its outdoor restaurants. The dark interior of the church still reflects the understated elegance of medieval times. Historically Vernazza was not only a village of wine-growers but an important seafaring city as well: it has the only natural sheltered harbour in the area. The inhabitants fought many wars in the 12th and 13th centuries as allies of the mighty republic of Genoa, which built fortifications around the village; today these are in ruins. As you can see from the colourfully painted entrances — some of them with reliefs — the people here were always quite wealthy, more so than in the neighbouring villages.

**Corniglia** is the only village of the Cinque Terre not on the coast: it lies on a ridge at a height of about 100m. From here you enjoy far-reaching views across the sea. It does not have a harbour, only a small rocky bay, reached by a long flight of steps — the 'Via alla Marina'. It gives the impression of being a mountain, rather than a seaside village. Corniglia is more remote and less crowded than its neighbours; it has no big hotels or posh restaurants. The heart of the old village is a cosy piazza shaded by plane trees and the umbrellas of two bars and a restaurant. The piazza is the sort of 'living room' of the little village, where everybody knows everybody else. In the daytime it's crowded with hikers having a break on their way from Vernazza to Manarola; in late evening it changes to a place of quiet contemplation. The church of SAN PIETRO at the exit from the village dates from the 14th century. The fine marble rose window is original, but the interior has been rebuilt in baroque style.

The colourful cube-like houses of **Manarola** are either piled up on a rocky outcrop above the water or lined up close together along the sides of a narrow valley — both settings are very picturesque. The inhabitants had to use every inch of ground to build their charming village, since it's encircled by steep slopes. Manarola was probably founded in the 12th century. In the Middle Ages there used to be many olive mills in the surroundings. Today olive-growing is still important, but Manarola's first claim to fame is that it's the Cinque Terre's white wine centre. The steeply terraced surrounding vineyards have the best grapes in the region. The central lane of the village is lined with shops selling local wine and olive oil. The parish church of SAN LORENZO at the upper edge of Manarola is a medieval gem. It has a beautiful 14th-century rose window and some 15th-century paintings inside.

**Riomaggiore** is probably the oldest of the villages. The name means 'larger river' and comes from the river that runs underneath the main street. Eleven bridges crossed the river before a street was built over the water in modern times. This village has no central square. Like neighbouring Manarola, it seems to be squeezed in between the steep slopes. Its centre lies on both sides of the main street leading up the hill. The picturesque highlight is the small horseshoe bay, where little wooden fishing boats rock on gentle waves. Rising steeply above are the clustered houses of the old village, warmly coloured in reds, yellows and oranges. Riomaggiore is connected to Manarola by Italy's most famous and most crowded walking trail, the VIA DELL'AMORE, a name which needs no translation. It is an easy panoramic one-kilometre-long stroll along the sea at the foot of steep cliffs. The SANCTUARY MADONNA DI MONTENERO high on the slopes above is one of the best viewpoints and picnic spots in the whole Cinque Terre.

## Getting about

There's a **local train** about every hour from La Spezia to Monterosso, Sestri Levante or Genoa; it stops at all five Cinque Terre villages. Then there are about 10 more connections a day from Riomaggiore and Monterosso by longer distance **regional trains**. A few **intercity trains** (reservations needed!) run between Monterosso and Pisa (4 a day; journey time 1h15min), Genoa (5 a day; 1h15min) and Milan (5 a day; 3h).

There are hardly any **buses**. There are buses from Monterosso to the Colla di Gritta pass above the town, from Vernazza's car park to the village, from Corniglia station to the village, from Manarola to Groppo/Volastra and from Riomaggiore to Bivio Monasteroli and Biassa. In winter only a few buses run.

From April to October **passenger boats** ply between Monterosso and Portovenere 4-7 times a day, docking at Vernazza, Manarola and Riomaggiore (but not Corniglia); for timetable/fares see www.navigazione golfodeipoeti.net.

During the walking season **parking** in the old centres is not allowed for non-residents. There are sign-posted parking areas outside the villages. But parking fees are high (about 12-15 € per day, 70-90 € per week).

## Walk planning

The first seven walks in this book cover the Cinque Terre proper. Walk 1, the classic coastal route from Monterosso to Riomaggiore, is nearly always very crowded. As are Walk 2 (Monterosso to Levanto) and Walk 5 (Riomaggiore to Portovenere). To avoid the crowds try one of the lesser-known routes.

**Out of area walks**: All routes to the south of Chiavari (Walks 1-18) can be done from all five villages as day trips. With an early start, even those further north (except for Walks 19, 26 and 27) are possible. And even these three are possible from Monterosso if one takes the first intercity towards Genoa at about 7 am.

## Accommodation

There is all sorts of accommodation in the five villages. In season early pre-booking is necessary. A good option is to take one of the many private rooms or B&Bs. **Monterosso** has the widest selection of hotels, but nearly all of them are very expensive. HOTEL AMICI★★★ in the old centre is one of the cheapest (double room from 100 €, www.hotelamici.it). At **Vernazza** simple HOTEL BARBARA★ at the harbour piazza or nearby GIANNI FRANZI★★ (www.giannifranzi.it) are relatively cheap options (double rooms from 65 €, some without own bath). **Corniglia** has no hotel but many private rooms for rent; for example see www.eterrasse.it or www.cecio5terre.com. There is also a new, fairly spartan youth hostel in the village (www.ostellocorniglia.com). At **Manarola** small and friendly CA D'ANDREAN★★★

(www.cadandrean.it) and MARINA PICCOLO★★★ (www. hotelmarinapiccola.com) are good options (from 110 €). The Manarola youth hostel is very good and very popular (www.hostel5terre.com, early booking advisable). At **Riomaggiore** LOCANDA CA'DEI DUXI★★★ has well-equipped rooms in a renovated small palazzo from 130 € (www.duxi.it). The village has a wide selection of private rooms bookable via agencies like Edi Vesigna (www.appartamenticinqueterre.net) or Dolce Vita (www.dolcevita5terre.com).

*Walk 1: descending from Prevo towards Corniglia*

# Walk 1: FROM MONTEROSSO TO RIOMAGGIORE — ALL THE CINQUE TERRE VILLAGES

**See photographs on pages 9, 15, 28-29 and opposite**
**Distance/time:** 12km/7.4mi; 4h45min
**Grade:** moderate, with an overall ascent/descent of about 550m/1800ft; two longer climbs each of 200m/650ft heading out from Monterosso and Vernazza. You have to be sure-footed between Monterosso and Vernazza; the path runs along narrow terraces.
*Important note:* At time of writing this walk was closed! The sections from Corniglia's railway station to Manarola and Manarola to Riomaggiore (the Via dell'Amore) were damaged by major landslides; reopening date is uncertain. The rest of the walk should reopen for the 2014 season: enquire at a Park information office at one of the railway stations (see page 16).
**Route-finding:** easy; red and white waymarks of National Park Route 2 all along (but note that *all* the walking routes in the Park have the same red and white markings…)
**Equipment:** as pages 12-13
**Refreshments:** many bars and restaurants in the five villages; simple bars en route at Prevo before Corniglia and at

Corniglia railway station
**Transport:** 🚍 local train or (from April to October) ⛴ boat — more expensive but much nicer than a train ride through dark tunnels.
**Map:** Tourist & Footpaths Map Cinque Terre/Portovenere/Palmaria Island (1:25,000, Ligurpress), available at the National Park offices in railway stations, 4 €
**Short walks:** The route can easily be divided into two walks: Monterosso – Vernazza (less than 2h) and Vernazza – Riomaggiore (2h45min).
**Entrance fee:** You need a permit to walk this route. Permits are available at railway stations, Park offices and various kiosks along the trail. It costs 6 € for one day, 9.70 € for two days. The full fee has to be paid even if you are just doing short sections. There is also a 'Carta Cinque Terre', costing 12 € per day or 23 € for two days (children from 4 to 12 years old pay half price). This card not only gives you permission to do the walk, but also allows free travel on all local and regional trains between La Spezia and Levanto as well as all local buses in the five villages.

This is *the* classic walk in the Cinque Terre National Park, connecting all five villages. The route follows old coastal paths high above the sea, skirts the edge of steep slopes, crosses small terraces of olive groves and vineyards or runs through shady holm oak forests. The views down to the blue sea and the villages with their yellow- and red-coloured houses clinging to each other are often breathtaking. So it is with good reason that this walk from Monterosso to Riomaggiore has become the most popular walking route in all Italy. From April to October there will be many, many walkers on the paths. So start very early to avoid the big crowds.

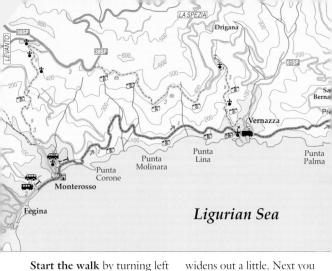

**Start the walk** by turning left when you leave **Monterosso's** RAILWAY STATION. Follow the pavement above the beach to a nearby road tunnel. Here take the pedestrian lane to the right: it skirts the steep slope guarded by an old WATCHTOWER, to come down onto the beach near the town centre. Keep to the right of the railway bridge and pass another beach, to arrive at the entrance gate of the HOTEL LA ROCA. Take the paved path with railings to the right here (RED AND WHITE WAYMARKS, ROUTE 2). Circling to the left you soon arrive at the KIOSK where you can buy your pass (**15min**).

Now you come into the typical Cinque Terre landscape, with its terraced vineyards and olive groves. The gradient soon becomes quite severe, as you climb a flight of natural stone steps through lush green vegetation. At the end of this ascent the path levels out and offers far-reaching views down to the sea. For a short way the path becomes very narrow as it runs alongside drystone walls *(take care here!)*. You pass behind a lone house, circle to the right, and cross a small old STONE BRIDGE. Then the path

22

widens out a little. Next you pass a small resting area (**1h**) which offers a superb view towards the steep cliffs of Vernazza. The path then runs along rocky slopes where subtropical agaves flourish, as it gradually looses height. You have views towards picturesque Vernazza. After descending 'staircases' and small lanes you come out on lively VIA ROMA in the old town centre of **Vernazza**.

The ongoing route to Corniglia starts opposite, at house number 50. The railway station is nearby at the upper end of Via Roma; while the lower end opens out to the IDYLLIC HARBOUR BAY with its outdoor restaurants and the medieval church of SANTA MARGHERITA (**2h**).

Leave Vernazza on the small stepped lane VIA M CARATTINO. Climbing out of the village, it skirts a MEDIEVAL TOWER, passes two bars with panoramic terraces and emerges on an open slope with succulents and agaves. Here you enjoy the famous view of Vernazza on its rocky promontory above the sea. Three minutes later, the path (now stone-laid), starts to climb more seriously through

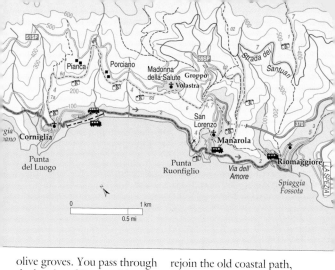

olive groves. You pass through the hamlet of **Prevo** with a simple bar on your right (**2h45min**). About two minutes higher up, the path starts its descent towards Corniglia which you can see ahead, stretched out on a ridge above the sea. Here you're walking a well maintained old cobbled mule trail lined by drystone walls. Beyond a bridge over a stream, the path crosses a small road on the outskirts of Corniglia. Keep ahead on a paved path through vineyards to the church of SAN PIETRO at the upper end of **Corniglia** (**3h25min**).

A short detour to the right leads to the cosy central piazza, but for Manarola you have to keep ahead on the lane to the left of San Pietro, soon crossing the station road emerging from the village. Go down the 383 steps of VIA LARDARINA, descending through lush vegetation to the sea. Turning left at the end of the steps you reach Corniglia's small RAILWAY STATION (**3h45min**).

Behind the building, take the subway below the railway and follow a track parallel to the seashore and a pebble beach. After a short steep climb you rejoin the old coastal path, walking above foaming surf and below steep cliffs overgrown with agaves and wild fennel. Skirting the promontory, suddenly **Manarola** appears, a beautiful image of colourful houses piled one atop the other like sugar cubes. Go down to the little harbour at the foot of the village, then take the main alley into the centre of the village. Cross the railway line and turn right. A short tunnel takes you to the RAILWAY STATION (**4h20min**).

To the left of the building steps lead up to the beginning of the famous VIA DELL'AMORE — easy walking on a flat, paved footpath protected by hand-rails. It runs along steep cliffs and offers fine sea views, but you meet masses of day-trippers here. In just under 20 minutes the Via dell'Amore ends at **Riomaggiore's** RAIL-WAY STATION. A short tunnel takes you to the centre of the village. Leaving the tunnel, turn right to cross under the rail lines and come to the beautiful small HARBOUR (**4h45min**). Passenger boats dock at the left (southern) end of the bay.

## Walk 2: FROM MONTEROSSO COLLA DI GRITTA TO LEVANTO — HIGH TRAILS ON THE COSTA SEMAFORO

See also photograph on page 9

**Distance/time:** 11km/6.8mi; 3h45min

**Grade:** moderate, with an overall ascent of 240m/790ft and descent of 540m/1770ft

**Route-finding:** easy; red and white waymarks of National Park Route 1; the diversion to Punta del Mesco is waymarked Route 10

**Equipment:** as pages 12-13

**Refreshments:** bars and restaurants in Monterosso and Levanto, simple bar en route after Punta del Mesco (overpriced!) and at the Hotel La Giada del Mesco

**Transport:** 🚌 from mid-March to the end of October there's a bus about every hour starting from Monterosso railway station and stopping at Piazza Garibaldi in the centre to Bivio Monterosso on the Colla di Gritta. For timetables see www.atpesercizio.it, line Monterosso–Vettora. 🚆 many local trains from Levanto to Monterosso

**Map:** as Walk 1, page 21

**Shorter walk: Monterosso railway station to Levanto.** 8km/5mi; 2h50min; moderate, starting with a steep ascent of 300m/1000ft; overall ascent/ descent 375m/1230ft. Leaving **Monterosso** RAILWAY STATION, turn right and walk parallel to the beach. At the foot of the hills, the road turns left and passes through an archway. Just behind it take the stepped path to the right (↑ PUNTA MESCO/LEVANTO, RED/WHITE WAYMARKS, ROUTE 10). It climbs steeply, circles the tower of an old villa and joins a small road (**15min**). Follow this uphill for some 10min to a left bend, then take the old mule trail to PUNTA MESCO on the right, rising steeply. Park repairs have spoiled the trail in some places, with modern concrete steps. But the views over Monterosso Bay keep improving as you climb. At a T-JUNCTION (305m) you join the main walk at the 1h48min-point near the medieval chapel of SANT'ANTONIO. Follow the main walk to the end.

Another walk with superb sea views, this popular hike follows the Costa Semaforo, the steep coast between Monterosso and Levanto. From the Colla di Gritta, a saddle on the hills to the north of Monterosso, the trail winds its way high on the slopes through typical Mediterranean vegetation — black pines, holm oaks, broom, heather, strawberry trees, myrtle and aromatic herbs. Halfway along, you overlook the whole Cinque Terre from the ruined lighthouse (*semaforo*) on the rocky Punta del Mesco promontory. Finally descending through farmland and olive groves, you arrive at the lively coastal town of Levanto. It offers good swimming on a long grey sand beach.

The classic route to Levanto starts from Monterosso railway station with an arduous uphill trail. The alternative route, which I've chosen for the main walk, begins at the Colla di Gritta; it's a little longer but requires less climbing and offers even better views. The two routes join near Punta del Mesco.

**Start the walk** at **Colla di Gritta**, from the small parking area next to the restaurant (325m). Wooden steps lead you to the start of a forest path (▮ LEVANTO, RED/ WHITE WAY-MARKS, ROUTE 1). It rises through pine wood on the northwestern side of the ridge, where the Portofino Peninsula comes into sight. Now stony underfoot, the trail dips through a HOLLOW (**15min**), then climbs steeply through pine and heather onto the hillock of **Monte Rossini** (465m; **40min**), where some benches invite you to take a break overlooking the entire Cinque Terre to the south. After a descent and a short re-ascent, the path emerges on an eroded slope and becomes deeply rutted. The descent, quite uncomfortable in places, ends at a junction on another pass, the **Colla dei Bagari** (360m; **1h10min**).

Keep left for ROUTE 1, which changes to a delightful trail. For a while it runs along the panoramic eastern slopes of **Monte Ve o Focone**. Later it undulates along the ridge, heading seaward, and sandy underfoot in places. In spring cistus and broom add some colour to the dark green of the macchia, which is brightened in autumn by the shining red and yellow fruit of the straw-berry bushes. Eventually the ruins of the chapel of Sant'Antonio appear straight ahead and an obvious trail crosses (325m; **1h45min**).

*Near Punta del Mesco*

The path continues downhill through Mediterranean macchia, crosses two small streams (normally dry) and runs along the steep coastal slope with good sea views. After a short climb through shady holm oak woods you go through the small hamlet **Case Carlo** (**2h45min**), ignoring a track off to the right. Once more you're high above the sea enjoying superb views. Bearing right uphill, the now-cobbled path joins a small road next to the HOTEL LA GIADA DEL MESCO (**3h10min**), which has a panoramic terrace bar.

From the hotel go down the road for about five minutes. On a right-hand bend take a path running straight ahead. It descends through olive groves, with far-reaching views towards the Portofino Peninsula. Becoming a stepped lane, then a small cobbled road, it takes you to the ruined CASTELLO DI SAN GIORGIO on the outskirts of Levanto. Immediately behind it take the stepped SALITA SAN GIORGIO down to the seashore. Walk 300m along the paved coastal promenade to the edge of **Levanto**'s old town centre, where you walk under the ARCHES OF THE OLD RAILWAY LINE (**3h35min**).

Carry on diagonally left on PIAZZA STAGLIENO beside a little pine tree park, go right on VIA DANTE ALIGHERI for 100m, then left into VIA GUISEPPE GARIBALDI. Leave the old town centre via an ARCH to the right, turn left at the next street, and after 50m right on VIA ROMA, leaving town. After crossing a dry streambed, steps on the left take you up to Levanto's RAILWAY STATION (**3h45min**).

A right turn here is the continuation of ROUTE 1 TO LEVANTO. But first make a short diversion to the left along ROUTE 10, to the superb viewpoint at Punta del Mesco: descending across some rocky furrows, you come to a fork in three minutes (**1h48min**). *(The Shorter walk coming up from Monterosso railway station joins here.)* Head right and go past the ruin of the medieval chapel of SANT'ANTONIO. A few minutes later you arrive at the more recent ruin of the LIGHTHOUSE (*semaforo*) on **Punta del Mesco**, standing at the edge of a steep rocky slope (314m; **1h55min**).

Retrace your steps to the 1h45min-point (**2h05min**). From here it's almost all downhill. The path for Levanto descends steadily through a forest of black pines and strawberry bushes. In some sections it's earthen or sandy, in other places stony. Around 15 minutes down from the saddle, keep to the right of a little STONE HUT, where high-priced snacks and drinks are sold in the walking season.

# Walk 3: FROM MONTEROSSO TO VERNAZZA VIA SOVIORE — HOLY PLACES ABOVE THE COAST

**Distance/time:** 9km/6mi; 3h30min

**Grade:** moderate; initial long ascent of 450m/1475ft; overall ascent/descent 550m/1800ft

**Route-finding:** easy; red and white waymarks, National Park Route 9 to Soviore, then 8b to Madonna di Reggio and finally 8 to Vernazza

**Equipment:** as pages 12-13

**Refreshments:** Bar-Ristorante Santuario Madonna di Soviore (good value, closed Tuesdays)

**Transport:** 🚆 local trains from Vernazza to Monterosso

**Map:** as Walk 1, page 21

**Short walk: Madonna di Soviore to Vernazza.** 6km/3.7mi; 2h. Start the walk at the 1h30min point; much easier than the main walk. 🚌 bus to Madonna di Soviore (departs Monterosso railway station at 8.36am and from the San Giovanni church on Piazza Garibaldi in the old town at 8.45. A second bus departs from Via Roma Carispe at the northern end of the town centre daily at 12.35. No buses November to mid-March. For timetables see www.atpeserci zio.it, line Monterosso–Vettora

Sanctuaries have stood on the wooded slopes high above the five villages of the Cinque Terre since medieval times — places of pilgrimage and spiritual retreat for centuries. This walk follows old cobbled paths to two of them, Madonna di Soviore above Monterosso and Madonna di Reggio above Vernazza. While the coastal paths are full of walkers, these higher routes are far more quiet. At a height of 400 to 600 metres, you enjoy wonderful views down to the sea and the villages of Monterosso and Vernazza.

Leaving **Monterosso** RAILWAY STATION, turn left. Follow the pavement above the beach to a nearby road tunnel. At its entrance take the pedestrian lane to the right. It skirts the steep coastal slope, guarded by an old WATCHTOWER, to come down onto the beach near Monterosso town centre. Pass

under the ARCHES of the railway. Turn left behind the black/white-striped medieval church of SAN GIOVANNI BATTISTA, to emerge in the small, cosy PIAZZA MATTEOTTI with its wine bars *(enotece)*. Leave the old town centre by heading right along narrow VIA VITTORIO EMANUELE. Join the main street, Via Roma, and follow this north out of town for five minutes, to the modern TOURIST OFFICE (**15min**). Take the stepped footpath off to the left here (☞ SENTIERO 9 PER SOVIORE, RED AND WHITE WAYMARKS).

Rising steeply, the trail passes to the left of the CASA DEI LIMONI (B&B), changing to an old cobbled trail. The gradient soon lessens and the path joins a concrete track (**30min**). Leave this immediately after the next right-hand bend, to pick up the old cobbled path again. It climbs steadily, first through a stand of oaks, then along an open slope with olive trees, where Monterosso Bay comes into view. Then you meet the Monterosso–Levanto road, the STRADA PROVINICIALE 38 (330m; **1h**).

Your ongoing path rises off the road some 30m to the left. After a short stretch of new pavement, the ancient stone-laid route reappears. A good 10 minutes above the road you pass a small CHAPEL and, after another 10 minutes, a small PINK DOME-SHAPED CHURCH in danger of collapsing. Soon you arrive at MADONNA DI SOVIORE (465m; **1h30min**), with fine views down to the sea. The sanctuary dates from medieval times. The large building to the left served as a pilgrim's hospice; today it houses a bar

*The approach to Vernazza*

and a simple but good restaurant.

Facing the church, take the broad track to the right. It narrows to a path, passes two new houses in three minutes, and joins a small road. Follow this uphill to the nearby Vernazza–Pignone road, where you turn right. Follow this road for a good 10 minutes; luckily there's not too much traffic. Ignore a concrete track off right where the road bends left, but after 100m turn right down a path (☞ MADONNA DI REGGIO; RED AND WHITE WAYMARKS, ROUTE 8*b*; 525m; **1h45min**).

The small path gradually loses height as it heads southeast through an area ravaged by fire in 1998. It is regenerating well, but the vegetation is still quite low in most places, offering little shade but superb views — first into Monterosso Bay overlooked by the Punta del Mesco promontory and later

down to the steep coast of Vernazza and Corniglia. Some 20 minutes down from the road the path drops steeply for 5 minutes. It then veers left in front of a ruin. After a short rise and another steep downhill section, you reach a depression with some drystone walls, where you have to climb over a small rock (**2h25min**). From here the path, rising gently, circles the hillside, offering a bird's-eye view onto Vernazza. Finally it joins the *PIGNONE– VERNAZZA ROAD* (440m; **2h 40min**). Follow this downhill for five minutes, then turn right on a sealed track leading to a nearby gate. Take a path descending left in front of the gate. Beyond a patch of wood you quickly come down to the large sanctuary of *MADONNA DI REGGIO* (330m; **2h50min**). If it's open, have a look at its colourful painted ceiling and its revered image of the Madonna.

Turn left behind the church and cross a small rest area shaded by old cypresses, holm oaks and plane trees. Turn sharp right opposite a *FOUNTAIN* and follow this lane downhill towards the sea ( *VERNAZZA, RED AND WHITE, WAYMARKS; ROUTE 8*). The lane changes to a beautifully cobbled path by some houses — a well-worn pilgrims' route. It descends gently, with fine views, passing old *TABER- NACLES* and a *CHAPEL*. These lead to the *CEMETERY* (**3h20min**) at the upper edge of Vernazza, where you enjoy a superb panorama over the small harbour bay. Bear left, descending a concrete track to the bottom of the valley, at the northern end of the village. Follow the valley road five minutes, to **Vernazza** *RAILWAY STATION*. From here it's five more minutes along the lively central lane to the picturesque *HARBOUR BAY* (**3h30min**).

## Walk 4: FROM CORNIGLIA TO MANAROLA VIA VOLASTRA — THE ART OF TERRAZZAMENTO

**See also photograph page 14**
**Distance/time:** 8km/5mi; 2h55min
**Grade:** moderate; some narrow terrace paths on which you have to be sure-footed
**Route-finding:** fairly easy; however some small turnings can be easily overlooked; red and white waymarks, National Park Routes 7a and 6d from Corniglia San Pietro to Volas-

tra, then 6 down to Manarola
**Equipment:** as pages 12-13
**Refreshments:** bar/restaurant at Volastra
**Transport:** 🚆 local train from Manarola to Corniglia
**Map:** as Walk 1, page 21
**Shorter walk:** about half an hour and 100m of ascent is saved by taking the 🚌 bus from Corniglia railway station into the village centre

Another popular walk in the Cinque Terre is the upper route from Corniglia to Manarola via Volastra. It offers impressive views over the famous vineyards dropping steeply 300m/1000ft to the sea. The local people have created a large network of drystone walls which follow the contours of the slopes, to support the terraces and prevent the soil from being washed away by the rain. This *terrazzamento*, the result of centuries of arduous toil, is a breathtaking work of landscape art.

Although this walk is relatively short, it should not be underestimated, as it starts with a steady climb from sea level up to 375m.

From **Corniglia** RAILWAY STATION follow the little-used road uphill to the village. After 150m there's a short-cut via stone steps on the right. This leads back onto the station road, which then bends left, offering a good view towards Manarola. At the edge of Corniglia VILLAGE, where the brick steps of VIA LARDARINA come up from the station, turn right on the narrow lane to SAN PIETRO: you can see its beautiful 14th-century rose window at the front. Some 30m before the church, your ongoing path to Volastra (ROUTE 7a) forks off to the right between a WATER TAP and a small SHRINE dedicated to the Madonna. But before heading right, a short detour into the

village centre is rewarding: turn left behind San Pietro, cross the square at the bus stop and carry on along the narrow lane leading between the houses. You soon enter the cosy little PIAZZA in the centre. Crossing straight over the square, to arrive at a panoramic balcony at the far end of the village (95m; **20min**). Return to Route 7a and start climbing through vineyards, now on a small cobbled mule trail. At the start there are good sea views, later the trail leads into a depression with olive trees. After some 30 minutes' climbing from Corniglia village, *be sure not to miss the turn-off for* ROUTE 6d: it forks off right after a left-hand bend (Both routes have red and white waymarks!). For a while the Route 6d path contours, then it starts rising in the shade of a wood which has grown up over old grape terraces. Twice the path seems to end in front of drystone walls, but you will find stone plates protruding from the walls, allowing you to climb up to a higher level, where the well-worn path continues. At the end of the ascent the villages of Manarola and Corniglia come into sight far below and the path swings left into a valley, passing a SPRING with drinking water pouring

*Steeply terraced vineyards, with Manarola in the background*

down from a rocky slope on the left. The path circles to the right and becomes an idyllic trail, easy underfoot.

Beyond a shady forest you arrive at the few houses of isolated **Porciano** (375m; **1h35min**). Walk to the right of the first house (respecting private property) and, behind it, stay on the same level, following a narrow path which passes to the left of a second house. After a left-hand bend the impressive image of the Volastra's extensive wine terraces, shown on page 31, appear. Today some of them are abandoned. The path contours easily, but still you must pay attention because it is very narrow as it skirts the upper edge of the steep vineyards. The views down to the sea are superb as you approach **Volastra**. This village of wine-growers is reached at the medieval church of MADONNA DELLA SALUTE (345m; **2h05min**).

Keep to the right of the church, following the flat main street eastwards between the houses. Around 100m after passing the bar-ristorante GLI ULIVI on your left, behind HOUSE NUMBER 4 and opposite a WATER TAP, take the stepped lane, descending southwards (ROUTE 6, RED AND WHITE WAYMARKS). Leaving the village, this reduces to a well-preserved old mule trail, carefully built from natural stones. Passing through terraced farmland with olive and fig trees, you come down to the small VOLASTRA–LA SPEZIA ROAD.

Take a path to the right, running parallel to the road, for 150m. You cross the side-road branching off for Manarola. The waymarked trail descends the left-hand side of the valley towards the sea. The trail rejoins the road at the upper edge of **Manarola**, and you soon pass the medieval church of SAN LORENZO (**2h40min**).

About 50 metres behind the church, take a path off right. It climbs some metres onto another path, contouring through vineyard terraces above the village. In front of a blocked-off gate (which prevents walkers from following a dangerous trail towards Corniglia), take some steps down to the left. Turn left in front of the CEMETERY. Turn right behind the walls, to arrive at a bar with a superb view onto the old village centre. A concrete footpath takes you down to the small HARBOUR. From here go uphill to the left, into the village, crossing the railway line. A short pedestrian TUNNEL connects the village to its RAILWAY STATION (**2h55min**).

## Walk 5: FROM RIOMAGGIORE TO PORTOVENERE — WHITE CLIFFS, BLUE SEA

**See photographs on pages 2, 4-5, 15 and cover**

**Distance/time:** 14km/8.7mi; 4h45min

**Grade:** moderate-strenuous; with an overall ascent/descent of 600m/1970ft. The steady climb of 500m/1650ft at the start is quite long, but not very steep. On some short, stony sections descending to Portovenere you must be sure-footed

**Route-finding:** quite easy; red and white waymarks throughout; National Park Route 3 up to the Colle di Telegrafo, then Route 1 to Portovenere. But remember that all routes in the Park are waymarked red/white!

**Equipment:** as pages 12-13

**Refreshments:** bar-ristorante at the Colle di Telegrafo (1h45min); bar next to Sant' Antonio Abate (2h05min, open May-Sept); Café Piccolo Blu in Campiglia serves drinks and some food (2h45min)

**Transport:** 🚤 the pleasant boat ride from Portovenere back to the Cinque Terre offers more superb views; the last departure from Portovenere is about 5pm. Half-hourly 🚌 bus from Portovenere to La Spezia, from there many 🚃 local trains to all five villages of the Cinque Terre

**Map:** as Walk 1, page 21

**Short walks:** The the first part of Walk 6 lets you split this walk into two; for buses from and to Biassa see Walk 6

**1 From Riomaggiore to Biassa** (easy-moderate, 2h 40min, 550m ascent/200m descent). Some 30m before the rest area next to SANT' ANTONIO ABATE turn left on waymarked ROUTE 4 which crosses Route 1 here. Keep left and go steadily downhill along a beautifully built old stone-stepped trail. About 30min down from Sant'Antonio Abate the small hillside town of **Biassa** (315m) is reached. Buses stop on the main road below SAN MARTINO church.

**2 From Biassa to Portovenere** (moderate, 3h20min, 550m ascent/200m descent). Follow Walk 6 from Biassa to SANT'ANTONIO ABATE, then finish with the main walk.

This is one of the most exciting routes on the Riviera di Levante. In the southeast the Cinque Terre coast ends with jagged limestone cliffs rising steeply from the sea. But at the start you walk through a less dramatic landscape, following an old pilgrims' trail up to a sanctuary in a splendid panoramic position. Then you head for Campiglia via small vineyard terraces and across a mountain range covered with pine, sweet chestnut, holm and cork oaks. Small Campiglia is another good vantage point, occupying the narrow ridge between the Gulf of La Spezia and the Ligurian Sea. Beyond here the trail skirts the edge of the cliffs, with fabulous views all the way down to beautiful Portovenere.

**Start the walk** at **Riomaggiore** RAILWAY STATION. Take the pedestrian TUNNEL to the old centre. Walk up the steep main road to the far upper end of the village, where you go

33

straight across a ROUNDABOUT. Follow a path directly ahead into a valley, immediately crossing a small stream (■ TELEGRAFO, RED AND WHITE WAYMARKS, ROUTE 3). This is the old pilgrims' route to the Sanctuary of Montenero. Walk along the valley floor for five minutes on a flat old cobbled footpath. The trail then starts rising to the right via steep steps, away from the stream.

About half an hour from Riomaggiore you cross a small road. Then the trail swings round to the right, steadily climbing through a pine forest. The gradient lessens and you pass a GROUP OF OLD HOUSES, nicely situated on open slope. A few minutes later you pass the end of a modern small single-track RACK RAILWAY used for transporting the grape harvest down to the wine cellars. Behind it, the path emerges on the grassy terrace of the SANTUARIO MADONNA DI MONTENERO (340m; **1h**). The views from here demand a pause. You overlook the whole Cinque Terre, from the steep Punta Mesco promontory near Monterosso to the Portovenere Peninsula.

Go up some steps at the back of the church (■ 3 TELEGRAFO). The path rises along a ridge. Some 10 minutes uphill from the sanctuary *take care not to go past* waymarked ROUTE 3 forking off right via a drystone wall. The narrow path runs nearly flat for a while, crossing old vineyard terraces and stands of wood, before it starts to rise again. After passing **Lemmen**, a group of old houses in a fine panoramic position (**1h25min**), the climbing becomes considerably stiffer. You rapidly gain height ascending stone steps and overgrown old terraces. Then the gradient eases as you cross a hillside densely covered with ferns. At the end of the rise you arrive at the bar/restaurant on the pass **Colle di Telegrafo** (516m; **1h45min**).

Turn right behind the building on a track running parallel to a small tarmac road on your left (■ PORTOVENERE, RED AND WHITE WAYMARKS, ROUTE 1). Walking along a flat wooded ridge, you come to a cobbled road. Follow this straight on for 150m, to cross waymarked ROUTE 4/4C (BIASSA–FOSSOLA). Some 30m further on you pass the little modern chapel of SANT'ANTONIO ABATE on the left (511m; **2h 05min**). Leave the road here, which starts descending to the right towards Schiara. Keep ahead on the earthen track of ROUTE 1, which keeps to the

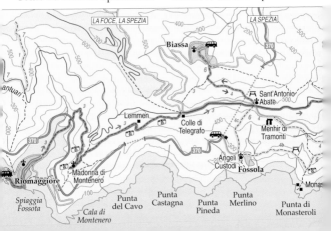

ridge for 10 minutes, rising a little, to a fork. Bear right here on a smaller track which soon narrows to a path and runs along the seaward hillside through a forest of mixed Mediterranean vegetation, including cork oaks. After 15 minutes the path begins to descend steeply. You pass to the left of a FARMHOUSE surrounded by a WALL. A good five minutes later you enter the village of **Campiglia**, where the Gulf of La Spezia comes into sight (380m; **2h45min**).

Walk straight on along the village ridge road for 50 metres. Then bear right, to go past the CHURCH and the café PICCOLO BLU. Carry on straight ahead. You pass the base of an old WINDMILL and enter a pine forest. Five minutes from Campiglia the path swings round to the left and descends to the CAMPIGLIA–LA SPEZIA ROAD. Follow this downhill for 250m, then turn right on a rocky path on the seaward-facing side of the hill. Within five minutes the path swings back to the road at a sharp left bend. Keep to the right of the tarmac, immediately picking up a descending path high above the sea. As you descend you enjoy fantastic views to the steep limestone cliffs that

dramatically punctuate the far end of the Portovenere Peninsula (photograph pages 4-5). Take care on some short sections with loose scree underfoot, especially when the ground is wet. After descending steeply for 30 minutes, ignore once again a small road on your left. Keep to the path straight ahead; it levels out and after five minutes finally joins the tarmac road (215m; **3h45min**).

Follow the road straight on for 300m, to a sharp right bend where you branch off left on a forest track. But after just 15m head right, uphill, on a steep path. Within three minutes this rejoins the road, which runs past a small quarry. On the next right-hand bend, keep ahead on an earthen track. It swings right and reduces to a path, with ever more eye-catching views of Portovenere Bay with Palmaria Island as a backdrop. About 10 minutes from the small road the path becomes steep and rough, in places rutted by erosion. *Walk carefully,* especially in wet weather. This rather uncomfortable downhill section ends in front of **Portovenere**'s CASTLE. A stepped footpath to the left of the castle walls takes you quickly down to the HARBOUR (**4h45min**).

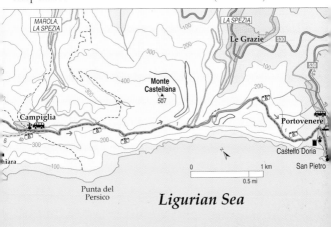

## Walk 6: CIRCUIT NEAR BIASSA AND CAMPIGLIA — STONY STEPS AND COBBLED MULE TRAILS

**Distance/time:** 10km/6.2mi; 4h15min

**Grade:** moderate, with an overall ascent/descent of 580m/1900ft; you must be sure-footed and have a head for heights

*Important note:* The path between Fossola and Campiglia is subject to landslides. Check at one of the railway station Park offices that it is open!

**Route-finding:** quite easy; red and white waymarks throughout; National Park Route 4 to Sant'Antonio Abate, then 4c and 4b to Campiglia; 4b, 4 back to Biassa

**Equipment:** as pages 12-13

**Refreshments:** Bar Piccolo Blu at Campiglia (behind the church)

**Transport:** 🚌 bus from Riomaggiore to Biassa (mid-Mar to Oct, daily at 9.30am); from Biassa back to Riomaggiore at 14.55, 16.52, 19.00. Or 🚌 bus from Piazza Brin in La Spezia (the big square 200m south of the railway station) to Biassa (on workdays at 7.41, 11.26, 12.26, 13.21; from Campiglia to La Spezia railway station on workdays at 13.00, 14.00, 15.35, 18.05). 🚆 many trains run from La Spezia to Riomaggiore; see www.atpcesercizio.it

**Map:** as Walk 1, page 21

**Short walks**

**1 Biassa—Campiglia** (6km/ 3.7mi; 2h45min; easy to moderate). Take a 🚌 to Biassa, either from Riomaggiore or La Spezia. Finish the walk at Campiglia and go by 🚌 to La Spezia.

**2 Strada Provinciale 370— Campiglia** (4km/2.5mi; 1h45min, easy to moderate). Take a 🚌 from Riomaggiore for Biassa or Monasteroli (the name of a bus stop, which is quite far away from the hamlet itself). Ascending the road from Riomaggiore leave the bus at the entrance to the SECOND ROAD TUNNEL, by a NATIONAL PARK BUILDING on the right selling local products (and with an overpriced bar). Walk along the panoramic, right-hand side of the road. In five minutes the tarmac ends at the 1h05min-point of the main walk. Follow it to Campiglia and go by 🚌 and 🚆 back to Riomaggiore via La Spezia.

---

The his walk takes you off the beaten track and into the isolated landscape of the 'Tramonti', a traditional wine-growing area to the south of Riomaggiore. On the way from Biassa to Campiglia, you pass through half-deserted hamlets with simply built small houses clinging to the slopes. Even today most of them are only accessible by the old cobbled footpaths. Elaborate flights of steep stone 'staircases' were built here to connect the vineyards high on the slopes with the landing stages down by the sea, so that the harvested grapes could be transported. They bring back to life the hardships the people faced in the past. Nowadays, thanks to the modern small single-track rack railways, the work has become much easier. At times this walk

follows small paths at the edge of steep terraces, so you must be sure-footed and have a head for heights. The views down to the sea are superb.

**Start the walk** in **Biassa** from the *CHIESA DI SAN MARTINO* (325m). Walk into the square behind the church and turn left under an *ARCH (RED AND WHITE WAYMARKS)*. The waymarks lead you along a small lane, and you leave the centre of the village. You cross a tarred square to its far end, then go straight ahead on *VIA DELLE POLLE*. Behind *HOUSE NUMBER 59*, turn right on a stepped footpath, climbing out of the village (*☞ SENTIERO 4*). The path soon changes to an earthen trail, which swings right between drystone walls. At the fork five minutes above Biassa, turn left.

You are now on the *OLD TRADING ROUTE* leading from La Spezia across the coastal mountain ridge to the vine-growing hamlets of the Tramonti. It has been painstakingly built from natural stones. Initially it rises with a modest gradient through a shady deciduous forest. Gradually the trail becomes a little steeper. Keep right at a junction, with a *PICNIC AREA* on your left. Some 100m further on you arrive on top of the ridge, where a small road waymarked as walking *ROUTE 1* crosses; to the left is the little modern chapel of

*SANT'ANTONIO ABATE* (511m; **40min**).

Cross the road and continue straight ahead on waymarked *ROUTE 4c*. Initially the path descends gradually through macchia and pine forest, still a magnificent old stone-laid trail. Some 15 minutes down from the ridge, you leave the forest and the route becomes steeper, contouring through vineyards facing the blue sea. At the first houses of **Fossola** (**1h05min**), you pass the end of a tarred road on the right. *(Short walk 1 joins here.)* A few minutes later

*Monasteroli staircase*

the now-cobbled trail goes past the small CHIESA DEGLI ANGELI CUSTODI, high on the slopes (265m; **1h10min**).

A short way downhill look out for the waymarks of ROUTE 4b: a small path turning off left, running along the upper edge of a terrace. It soon leads you between the few houses of Fossola, where you keep to the left, climb steeply for three minutes. Bear right to leave the hamlet on a small, almost flat path running along the steep coastal slope with its agaves. Far below, on a ledge pointing out into the sea, the reddish-coloured roofs of Monasteroli come into view. The path dips through a hollow with a REST AREA (TABLE), passing through a shady holm oak wood. After a short climb it meets a stepped footpath (**1h50min**).

This is the perfectly preserved OLD STAIRCASE TO MONASTE-ROLI. Women used to carry the harvested grapes down this airy trail to the boats, balancing heavy baskets on their heads. I suggest that you content yourself with the bird's-eye view down to Monasteroli that you have from here — both because of the steep ascent back up from the hamlet and the fact that the path from the hamlet to the sea has been destroyed by erosion. So turn left to climb the staircase, which soon changes to a less steep cobbled mule trail. On a left-hand bend, take a smaller path off to the right (⊪ CAM-PIGLIA, ROUTE 4b). It rises steadily through terraced vine-yards and holm oak woods. It meets another path in front of a big fountain, the FONTANA DI NOZZANO (330m; **2h15min**; drinking water).

Turn right here. Within three minutes the path joins a small tarred road. Follow this uphill for 100m then, on a bend to the left, take a path going straight ahead. This runs along open slopes above the scattered houses of **Schiara**, with fine sea views. A lovely path leads you through a patch of Mediterranean vegetation and vineyards. *Take care here;* for a short while the narrow path runs along the edge of a steep terrace! Following the way-marked trail you enter the village of **Campiglia**, situated on the ridge between La Spezia Bay and the open sea (380m; **2h45min**).

From Campiglia retrace your steps to the FONTANA DI NOZZANO (**3h10min**) and follow the stepped path uphill to the right (⊪ SANT'ANTONIO, BIASSA, ROUTE 4). It traverses a vineyard, offering fine views back to the cliffs of Palmaria Island. After crossing a single-track harvesting RACK RAILWAY it enters the forest. Ignore a path off left for Monasteroli and cross a track 100m further uphill. The trail, sometimes cobbled, sometimes earthen, climbs steadily up the wooded hillside. Where it joins a small road (475m; **3h30min**), you will find the 2.5 metre-high MENHIR DI TRAMONTI on the left — probably a place of worship during the Bronze Age. Opposite is an arched shelter and a stone bench, where the women could put the heavy grape-laden baskets down and take a break.

The road climbs gradually through a sweet chestnut forest back to SANT' ANTONIO ABATE (**3h40min**). From here take you outgoing route back to **Biassa** (**4h15min**).

## Walk 7: FROM SAN BENEDETTO TO MANAROLA — BEYOND THE RIDGE

**Distance/time:** 14km/8.7mi; 5h15min

**Grade:** moderate, with an overall ascent of 550m/1800ft and descent of 780m/2600ft

**Route-finding:** needs attention! There are many forks, and waymarks are rare.

**Equipment:** as pages 12-13

**Refreshments:** none en route

**Transport:** 🚌 from La Spezia railway station (Via Fiume) to San Benedetto: runs workdays at 7.30, 8.37, 9.30 (not Sat), 10.00, 10.37, 11.05, 11.37; on Sundays only at 9.15, 11.15. Take any bus for Ricco del Golfo, Padivarma, Borghetto or Brugnato; alight after passing the side road off left with many blue signposts for nearby villages (Porcale, Carpena, Codeglia, etc.) and a white sign 'Campo Sportivo'; journey time 12 minutes; for timetables see www.atcesercizio.it. To return 🚆 local train from Manarola to La Spezia

**Map:** as walk 1, page 21

**Alternative: Direct descent from Corniolo ridge to Manarola** (12km/7.4mi; 4h50min; fairly strenuous). Before the flat VIA DELL'AMORE was built, there was only a very steep path between Manarola and Riomaggiore, which are separated by the Corniolo ridge. This VIA BECCARA was reopened 2013 by the National Park administration, which also fixed some ropes and railings for the safety of the walkers. The trail is not really dangerous, but because it is so steep and narrow you have to be absolutely sure-footed and careful. At the far end of **Corniolo ridge** (the 4h15min-point in the main walk), turn back the way you came and go through a SECOND METAL GATE 15m below the gate you went through before arriving at the viewpoint. One through the gate the path turns sharply left (BLUE SIGNPOST FOR MANAROLA). Initially protected by a wooden railing, it descends, sometimes via small stone steps and later alongside very steep terraces. The route offers superb views down to Manarola nestled in a valley by the sea. After entering **Manarola** village (**4h40min**) turn right for SAN LORENZO church. From there follow the main walk to the RAILWAY STATION (**4h50min**).

A mountain range rising between 600 and 800 metres protects the vine-growing villages of the Cinque Terre from the cooler climatic influences of the high Apennines. This ridge separates the Mediterranean coast from the more nordic-looking mountains of the interior. It's *terra incognita:* hardly any hikers cross this ridge, where forgotten villages and hamlets hide in vast deciduous forests. Even this guide mostly keeps to the coast — except for the first half of this walk. We start from the small village of San Benedetto northwest of La Spezia, from where a long but mostly easy climb through oak and sweet chestnut woods takes us across the ridge. The descent to the sea follows little-used paths, with superb views over the whole Cinque Terre.

**Start the walk** from the BUS STOP in the village of **San Benedetto** (225m). Walk up the main road some 30m then, behind BAR-ALIMENTARI MATTEO'S turn left on VIA ANTONIO GRAMSCI, to climb out of the village on this small side road. At a junction five minutes further on, keep right, after 50m coming to a little white CHURCH. Opposite, by a BOARD WITH A WALKING MAP, take a grassy trail off right. It leads into a small valley, passes some wooden HUTS and enters a shady damp forest, narrowing to a path. Here you cross a stream on a stony BRIDGE. The path rises away from the valley floor alongside moss-covered drystone walls, to meet the SAN BENEDETTO–QUARATICA ROAD (20min).

Keep ahead along the road for 30m, then take an old stepped path rising to the left through oak wood (RED AND WHITE WAYMARKS UP TO QUARATICA MAIN CHURCH). About five minutes further up you meet the QUARATICA ROAD once more. Take steps up to the embankment opposite, to come onto the old mule trail heading for the village. It rises gently at the edge of olive tree terraces, offering far-reaching views to the high Apennines of Tuscany and takes you to the eastern group of houses in the relatively unspoilt old village of **Quaratica**. Keeping up steps and beneath some arches, you meet the main village 'street', the VIA SAN ROCCO — too narrow for cars. Turn left and pass a small NICHE with a WATER TAP decorated with an amphora (drinking water), to enter the western part of the village. Beyond another arch, keep right and go uphill under-

neath dark old vaulted passageways. At the VILLAGE CHURCH you join the tarmac road VIA MATTEOTTI coming up from San Benedetto (375m; **40min**).

Follow Via Matteotti 150m downhill *(no waymarks)*. At the end of a sharp left-hand bend take some steps down to the right. A small path then takes you to the right of a STEEP DITCH alongside moss-covered old walls. At the valley bottom, three minutes down from the road, the path swings left and rises gently from the ditch. Crossing a forest of sweet chestnut you arrive at a larger path with RED AND WHITE WAYMARKS (**55min**).

Follow this only 20m to the left, then fork right on an *unmarked* path. This small but distinct trail contours the northeastern slope of thickly wooded **Monte Due Fratelli**. You pass overgrown old terrace walls and gnarled chestnut trees. Leaving the wood (**1h10min**), the view opens out over the Gulf of La Spezia to the steep limestone mountains of the Alpi Apuane. The path swings right along the upper edge of olive groves and becomes concreted. At a junction, turn left downhill, to follow a dark vaulted lane through the nearby village of

**Porcale Superiore** and come to the end of a tarmac road (400m; **1h25min**).

Follow the road out of the village and turn right at a junction. Keep to the tarmac road for 15 minutes, rising gently, with a deep valley on the left. Arriving at **Codeglia** hamlet (429m; **1h45min**) turn right on a footpath which rises to the left of the colourful line of houses, then cuts through a small tunnel passageway (*RED AND WHITE WAYMARKS, ROUTE 02A*). Past the houses, you come onto a small path, sealed initially, which rises away from the village and swings right. It's a stiff climb through a sweet chestnut forest. After a sharp bend to the left, 10 minutes up from Codeglia, the gradient gradually lessens. Turn left at a T-junction (**2h05min**; *RED AND WHITE WAYMARKS, ROUTE 02*). The disused grassy forest track leads you up towards the ridge separating the Cinque Terre from the hinterland. Ignore an uphill path on the right. About five minutes further up, the trail joins the end of a forest track (**2h15min**).

Follow this straight on for just 20m, then turn right on a path (*A FEW WAYMARKS OF ROUTE 02*). It climbs steeply west through a forest of sweet chestnut. In late summer the ground is covered with a great variety of mushrooms. Some 10 minutes up, negotiate some large fallen trees by swerving left. At the *TOP OF THE RIDGE* you meet an obvious crossing trail (725m; **2h35min**). From now it's almost all downhill. Turn left, leaving the steep, direct Route 02 for Manarola. Instead take waymarked *ROUTE 1* which keeps to the ridge for a while. It passes a small *CAVE* on the left and starts descending along the seaside slope. Leaving the wood you get a bird's-eye view onto Manarola. A few minutes later you arrive at the saddle **Passo La Croce**, where several walking routes join (635m; **2h55min**).

*Around Quaratica*

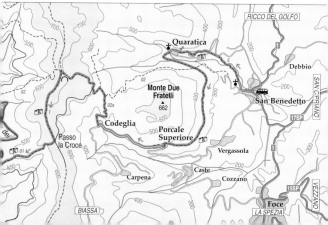

Turn right on ROUTE 01 FOR RIOMAGGIORE, which carries on downhill, away from the ridge (RED/WHITE WAYMARKS). The path is quite steep and stony underfoot at first. But only five minutes down from the saddle it changes to a lovely old mule trail, descending gently via sweet-scented pines with far-off views north to the steep coast of Monterosso. Finally it joins the STRADA DEI SANTUARI, the 'Road of the Sanctuaries' (405m; **3h20min**).

Not a tarmac road, but an old earthen track closed to motorised traffic, this connects the sanctuaries above the five villages. Leave Route 01 here and follow the STRADA to the right (no waymarks). Avoiding steep climbs, it contours round the slopes. After about 25 minutes of easy walking, the *strada* rises slightly onto the prominent **Corniolo ridge** (**3h45min**). A track turns off to the left here and, just 15m further on, waymarked Route 02 also turns off left.

Take the track, which descends the left side of the ridge (no waymarks). A good five minutes down you pass two houses in a splendid panoramic position on the right. Behind a third house, on the left, the track reduces to a path. Keep straight ahead along the ridge, which reveals fabulous sea views. The path zigzags down to the right of vineyards, passes an open SHELTER for farming machinery on the right, then levels out. Keep straight on and pass a hillock capped by a SMALL MAST to the left. Go through a metal gate and proceed to the far end of the ridge, a splendid VANTAGE POINT high above the sea (205m; **4h15min**).

Retrace your steps to the SHELTER for farming machinery and turn left just behind it. *(But the Alternative walk leaves the outward route at the vantage point.)* For the main walk, follow a well-built path along the slope, to the left of pine woods. Five or so minutes later the trail narrows and circles round to the left along the upper edge of a vineyard. After going through a gate you meet the path of ROUTE 02. Follow it downhill for only 100m then, about 40m below an OLD STONE HUT, turn right on a level path (no waymarks). It runs along the lower end of a vineyard and soon joins the VOLASTRA–LA SPEZIA ROAD at the foot of **Groppo** village (**4h45min**).

Follow the road downhill for five minutes. About 50m past an old olive oil mill ('FRANTOIO ANTICO MULINO'), descend some steps to the left. Continue down the valley on a cobbled mule trail, parallel to a stream (RED AND WHITE WAYMARKS, ROUTE 6). It crosses the road coming down from Groppo, runs parallel to it for 150m, then crosses the SIDE ROAD FOR MANAROLA (**5h**). The still-waymarked trail descends the left side of the valley. At the upper edge of **Manarola** it rejoins the road, which soon passes the church of SAN LORENZO (**2h40min**). Carry on down the central street, to the entrance of the short TUNNEL to the RAILWAY STATION (**5h15min**).

# La Spezia Bay

## Gulf of Poets

*Portovenere*

**A** t the southeastern end of Liguria a wide bay opens out between two promontories, with the busy naval town of La Spezia in the middle. All around, a ring of green mountains forms a scenic backdrop. In the 19th and early 20th centuries this area was one of the most popular destinations on the Italian Riviera for people fleeing from the cold dark winters of northern Europe. Among them were quite a few well-known writers, who temporarily settled in this unspoilt Mediterranean idyll — Lord Byron, Mary and Percy Bysshe Shelley, John Keats and D H Lawrence. That's why the bay of La Spezia later acquired the nickname 'Gulf of Poets'.

Today La Spezia, with nearly 100,000 inhabitants, is the second biggest town in Liguria and has completely lost its traditional small fishing village charm.

Because of its sheltered harbour it was developed as Italy's largest naval base. In the 20th century, La Spezia's shipyards saw the growth of the weapons and metal-working industries. Even thought many factories have closed over the past decades, La Spezia still lives from industry and the navy — a complete contrast to the charming villages of the Cinque Terre.

But **La Spezia** *does* have something to offer the visitor — the opportunity to see Italian everyday life at first hand. The lively inner city around VIA DEL PRIONE, a pedestrian zone, has many small shops, bars, food stalls and restaurants. A big colourful OUTDOOR MARKET for vegetables, fruit and fish is held from Monday to Saturday on PIAZZA CAVOUR in the centre. La Spezia also has a few interesting little museums, like the fine arts MUSEO AMADEO LIA or the CAMeC, the museum of contemporary art. SAN GIORGIO CASTLE hosts archaeological exhibits from Roman times and the 'Lunghiana Steles', an unusual collection of menhirs over 3000 years old.

Unlike La Spezia, **Portovenere** at the extreme southwestern tip of the Gulf has kept all its Mediterranean charm. It is one of the most beautiful little towns on the whole Italian Riviera. Dominated by a LARGE CASTLE, its multicoloured old facades face out to the small island of **Palmaria** rising from the sea, thus forming a sheltered harbour bay. In the 12th century the Republic of Genoa transformed the small town, which guarded the entrance to the Gulf, into a strong fortress against the hostile Maritime Republic of Pisa. You enter the old town via a 12th-century gate in the fortified walls to walk along dark and narrow VIA CAPPELLINI, which crosses the historic centre. The church of SAN LORENZO below the castle is a fine example of medieval religious architecture, as is SAN PIETRO church at the far end of the town. The latter, shown on page 2, sits in a splendid location on a rocky outcrop above the sea in the shade of vertical limestone cliffs. This place has been settled since ancient times. Portovenere means 'Harbour of Venus'. The Romans believed that Venus, the Goddess of Love, rose from the sea here.

As at Portovenere, the harbour bay of **Lerici** on the eastern shore of the Gulf is overlooked by a massive MEDIEVAL CASTLE. It was built by the Republic of Pisa, which was definitively defeated in 1284 by the Genoese armada. The castle houses the MUSEO GEO-PALEONTO-LOGICO, with models of dinosaurs and a seismic simulation room. Below the castle the little historic centre with its narrow alleyways clings to the slopes. The town attracts a fashionable clientele: in the small harbour the few remaining simple fishing boats have to share space with many yachts. A long crescent bay of sandy beaches lined by elegant villas extends from Lerici west towards neighbouring **San Terenzo**, with its smaller Genoese castle. But from there to La Spezia the beauty of the landscape has been destroyed by over-development.

Tiny **Tellaro**, at the southeastern end of the Gulf, is a real gem. The houses cluster together on a rocky ledge above the foaming sea. Only narrow lanes, small passageways and steep steps descend through the centre to the sea, where little SAN GIORGIO CHURCH stands guard above the lovely harbour bay. Tellaro has no sights — it is a sight in itself. It's a quiet, charming place with just one cul de sac street. It has pleasant beaches and unspoilt natural surroundings. The sparsely inhabited rough coast south of the village and the inland hills cloaked in pristine Mediterranean holm oak woods offer some good hiking. Thanks to the regulations of the **Montemarcello-Magra Nature Park**, the area is protected from further development.

To the east of the **Montemarcello** hills, the lively historic centre of **Sarzana**, spreading out along the **Magra Plain**, is worth a visit. The main sights are the medieval cathedral SANTA MARIA ASSUNTA and the massive 15th-century castle FORTEZZA DI SARZANELLO on the hills above the city.

## Getting about

Fast **Frecciabianca** and **intercity** trains leave La Spezia to the north for Monterosso (5 a day), Levanto (7 a day), Sestri Levante (8 a day), Chiavari (11 a day), Rapallo (11 a day), Santa Margherita Ligure (5 a day), Genova (13 a day; journey time 1h15min-1h40min), Milan (9 a day, journey time 3h15min) and Turin (3 a day); to the south for Pisa (13 a day; journey time 1h), and Rome (8 a day, journey time 3h30min-4h15min). About every hour there is a **local** or **regional train** to Monterosso/Sestri Levante and to Sarzana/Pisa. There are regional trains for Parma (where you would change for Bologna) about every two hours.

**Buses** run from La Spezia via San Terenzo and Lerici to Sarzana (half-hourly or every 15 minutes as far as Lerici on workdays) and to Portovenere (half-hourly). Buses to Lerici/Sarzana stop on Via Fiume in front of the railway station, those to Portovenere five minutes away, to the north of the big market hall (at Corso Cavour 140). There's a bus from Lerici to Tellaro about every hour except for Sunday mornings.

From April to October there are **boats** 3-7 times a day from La Spezia and Lerici to Portovenere; for the timetable see www.navigazionegolfodeipoeti.it.

In summer, especially at weekends, there are long **traffic jams** and little parking around Portovenere and Lerici.

## Walk planning

There are five walks in this book around La Spezia Gulf. Walk 8 (Palmaria Island), 9 (Lerici to Tellaro) and 10 (Tellaro to Lerici) are quite easy, whereas Walk 11 (Tellaro to Bocca di Magra) and Walk 5, which ends at Portovenere, are more demanding.

**Out of area walks:** If you are staying at Lerici, Tellaro or Portovenere you could also do most of the walks further north. But they would involve quite a bit of time on buses and trains, so I would not recommend any day trips further north than Sestri Levante.

## Accommodation

**La Spezia** is not ideal as a holiday base, but if you need accommodation, HOTEL VENEZIA★★★ on Via Paleocapa next to the railway station is a good option (www.hotel venezialaspezia.it), as is the more expensive palazzo-likeFIRENZE E CONTINENTALE★★★ opposite (www.hotel firenzecontinentale.it). Those seeking peace and quiet should head for secluded **Tellaro**. Here middle-range MIRAMARE★★ is a good choice (from 100 €, www.mira maretellaro.com). It's near the old village centre, as is the simple ALBERGO DELLE ONDINE, which is only 1-star but well kept and good value (from 70 €, www.albergo delleondine.com). **Lerici** has quite a few hotels, among them the panoramic DORIA PARK★★★ on the slopes above the harbour (from 120 €, www.doriahotels.com). **Portovenere** has just a few expensive hotels. The small ALBERGO GENIO★★, built against the old town's wall, is among the less expensive places to stay (from 100 €, www.hotelgenioportovenere.com).

## Walk 8: ISOLA PALMARIA — A WALK ON THE ISLAND

**See also photographs on pages 2, 43 and cover**
**Distance/time:** 7km/4.3mi; 2h20min
**Grade:** easy-moderate; overall ascent/descent 280m/920ft; on the short steep descent/ ascent to/from Cala Pozzale you have to be sure-footed
**Route-finding:** easy; red and white waymarks, signposts and trail numbers throughout
**Refreshments:** restaurant Locanda Lorena near the landing stage at Terizzo (quite expensive); simple bar/ restaurant at Cala del Pozzale during the swimming season

**Equipment:** as pages 12-13
**Transport:** 🚢 8-10 ferries a day from Portovenere to the landing stage on the north shore of Palmaria; for time-tables see www.comune. portovenere.sp.it, then click on 'Vivere a Portovenere', then on 'Usare mezzi di trasporti'. From mid-June to mid-Sept some boats go directly from La Spezia harbour to Palmaria Island. Boats sail from Porto-venere to Riomaggiore from Apr to Oct at 8.50, 10.00, 11.00, 12.00, 15.00, 17.00; timetables/fares see page 19
**Map:** as Walk 1, page 21

T hree little islands sit out to sea in the Gulf of La Spezia. But only one of them, the Isola di Palmaria close to Portovenere, is big enough to merit its own walk. There's only a handful of houses on the island, which is nearly free of road traffic. The gentle northern slopes, rising to a maximum height of 186 metres, are covered with Mediterranean macchia, at its most

colourful when blooming in spring and early summer. The island's more barren southern side ends at vertical limestone cliffs dropping off into a foaming sea. This pleasant circuit around the Isola di Palmaria not only offers fine sea views but good swimming at the stone- and pebble beach of Cala del Pozzale.

**Start the walk** at the LANDING STAGE on **Isola di Palmaria**: go ahead 30m to a T-junction and turn left on a trail parallel to the shore. Some three minutes later you pass the walls of a MARITIME RESEARCH STATION on the left, cross a small pebble beach and pass in front of RISTORANTE LORENA. Carry on along wooden planks to the small harbour square of **Terizzo**, a group of houses by the sea (**10min**). Look out for a pole with walkers' signs on the right, where some steps lead uphill (☛ STRADA DEI CONDANNATI 1.8KM, RED AND WHITE WAYMARKS).

You join a path swinging left, then meet a small road. Follow it uphill for 100m, then turn right on ROUTE 3. This is the STRADA DEI CONDANNATI, the 'convicts' street', which connected Terizzo harbour with the big 19th-century prison, Forte Cavour, at the top of the island. Cobbled and shaded, this old trail zigzags uphill, crosses the island's small asphalt road, and gains height along a shrub-covered ridge. You enjoy fine views back down to the multicoloured façades at Portovenere harbour. At a Y-fork 10 minutes up from the road, bear right, ignoring the left turn signposted for Pozzale. Passing through a wood, the trail becomes a little steeper. At the END OF THE ASCENT (**40min**), turn right. The path widens to a track running along the walls of FORTE CAVOUR. The castle/

fort was built around 1860, but is today in ruins, all overgrown by trees, thorny scrub and ivy.

From the end of the fortress follow the small tarred road coming up from Terizzo some 150m uphill, to **Colle Montroni** (175m; **45min**). Here on the saddle, some 50m in front of the compound gate of a white transmitter building on the hilltop, you'll find a picnic table on the left. Take the path descending left behind the table and bench, initially dropping steeply through a patch of wood (☛ POZZALE 35MIN, RED AND WHITE WAYMARKS, ROUTE 1). Go downhill over rocky ground and across open terrain with views to the sea. Around 10 minutes down from Colle Montroni ignore a left turn to Terizzo. The trail leads to the lowest point of a rocky ridge, where the impressive vertical cliffs of **Cala Grande** come into sight to the north (**1h05min**).

From here the path turns left across the stony ridge and descends steeply, swinging left to a small RUIN. Veer right in front of the ruin. Take care here as you descend to the sea over some loose scree. Follow a flat trail along the shore for five minutes, to **Cala del Pozzale** (**1h20min**).

Behind the simple bar/ restaurant building, only open in summer, bear left into a small short valley with two palm trees. Take the way-

marked path behind them, rising steeply inland via steps. A rope fixed to the trees gives hold. Ten minutes up from the *cala*, turn right at a T-junction. A pleasant path, flat and easy underfoot, runs along a terrace with an old stone wall on the left and fine views over the Gulf of La Spezia. After a left turn the path starts descending. For a short while it becomes a little uncomfortable on rocky ground. You join a track and in five minutes meet the island's small road. Follow it 250m downhill to your outgoing route and retrace your steps via **Terizzo** to the LANDING STAGE (**2h20min**).

## Walk 9: FROM SAN TERENZO TO TELLARO VIA LERICI — GULF OF POETS

See also photograph on pages 58-59

**Distance/time:** 10km/6.2mi; 3h30min

**Grade:** easy-moderate; overall ascent/descent of 460m/1500ft

**Route-finding:** in spite of red/white waymarks all along the route, you have to be attentive because there are many forks

**Equipment:** as pages 12-13

**Refreshments:** two bars en route at Pugliola

**Transport:** 🚌 bus from Tellaro to Lerici (workdays about every hour, Sundays only 7 buses). Then bus to San Terenzo (every 15 to 30min, Line Sarzana–Lerici–La Spezia railway station–Fossiterme).

**Map:** 4LAND, Sheet 141 Bassa Val di Magra/ Parco di Montemarcello-Magra (CAI Sarzana, 1:25,000)

The famous English writers who in 19th and 20th centuries temporarily settled around the Gulf of La Spezia — the 'Golfo dei Poeti' — appreciated the beauty of Mediterranean landscapes. Even today this vast Gulf with its small one-time fishing villages, secluded bays, pine forests and olive groves, has kept its appeal, despite being so much more heavily populated than in days gone by. The first half of this easy walk crosses the hills above the large crescent-shaped bay to Lerici, overlooked by its medieval castle. For this half you're mainly walking along typical Ligurian paved footpaths (*crosa* or *creuza*), passing through small villages with colourful houses. The second half of the walk leads into more open countryside, where you enjoy splendid views across the Gulf. Your final destination is the highly picturesque tiny coastal village of Tellaro.

**Start the walk** from centre of **San Terenzo** at the far western end of the bay, at the foot of the *CASTLE HILL*. Walk along the seashore promenade parallel to the coastal road. You pass the main *CHURCH* and white *VILLA MAGNI* on the left, in 1822 the home of Percy Bysshe Shelley and his wife Mary, the author of *Frankenstein*. The promenade then curves round a prominent hill at *VILLA MARIGOLA*. Just past its entrance gate follow a side-road for some 20m, then turn left on a shady path (▸-BAGNOLA, RED AND WHITE WAYMARKS, ROUTE 457). It climbs parallel to the old wall of Villa Marigola to the upper gate of the compound. Continue on the small road leading off the path, to cross a bypass road on a bridge and come to a fork in front of a small *SHRINE* to the Madonna (**20min**).

Take waymarked *ROUTE 456B* to the right. A walkway now takes you through the old hamlet of **Bagnola**. At the end of the row of houses join a cobbled mule trail heading left. Climbing through olive groves this meets a small road where you continue straight ahead. At the following road junction go uphill to the right, into the village of **Solaro**. You meet the

*San Terenzo*

road for Pugliola in front of a BUS SHELTER (**35min**).

Take the stepped footpath some metres to the left, the VICOLO CORTESE (☞ PASSO DELLA CISTERNA, RED AND WHITE WAYMARKS, ROUTE 456). It's a stiff but shady climb. Veering left, the old path levels out briefly through reeds, then starts gaining height again. The ascent ends at a T-junction (165m; **50min**); to the right is a small meadow with a RUIN and a WOODEN TABLE, a good resting place with fine views down into Lerici Bay.

Turn right at the T-junction (☞ AVG ALTA VIA DEL GOLFO, BOCCA DI MAGRA, RED AND WHITE WAYMARKS). This lovely path contours along the ridge for just three minutes, then zigzags down inland through a shady deciduous forest. Ignore a trail coming up from the valley to the left; keep right. A concrete footpath between old walls and then a lane take you up to the edge of **Pugliola** village, where you keep straight ahead on VIA RINALDI. The small road curves slightly to the left, to meet the main

road in the centre (VIA MILI-TARE; **1h05min**); a first bar is 50m to the left.

Cross Via Militare, continue along VIA G CASINI for just 50m, then take a stepped footpath uphill to the right of Bar Pugliola. This crosses G Casini again and we walk through the village on this typical Ligurian pavement. Ignore the main CHURCH on the right and carry on straight ahead along VIA D CARRO. Just before joining the main road at the far end of Pugliola, turn right downhill on a brick stepped footpath, SALITA CANNATA (☞ LERICI CENTRO, RED AND WHITE WAYMARKS, ROUTE 460). It joins a small road by some cypresses. Always keep straight ahead, to pick up another stepped footpath descending to Lerici Bay, full of boats and yachts. Follow the footpath by the seashore to PIAZZA GARIBALDI at the foot of the castle hill in **Lerici** (**1h30min**).

Cross the square diagonally left. Then take the steps of VIA SEVERINO ZANELLI to the right of TRATTORIA AL CANTIERE. The

51

walkway leads uphill through the old part of the town to the CASTLE, where you have fine views across Lerici Bay to San Terenzo.

Retrace your steps for some 100m and turn right on VIA TAGLIATA (⌐ MARALUNGA). The small concrete lane leads uphill to a street. Follow this to the left for 250m, to join the LERICI–TELLARO ROAD (**1h 45min**). Turn right and after 50m take the *second* path off left (⌐ TELLARO/BOCCA DI MAGRA, RED AND WHITE WAY-MARKS, ROUTE 3). The path, initially tarmac, rises gently away from the road. Entering a patch of wood it crosses a small stream and becomes steeper. At a fork, turn left on some wooden steps. Behind a LONE RED HOUSE you cross a tarmac track ending at a gate and take some steps leading to your on-going trail. It descends briefly into a small cultivated valley

where agaves and cactus flourish, then swings left, uphill again. At a fork where waymarked Route 464 comes down from Serra on the left (**2h10min**), turn right and keep to ROUTE 3.

The path crosses an olive grove and meets a concrete track. Follow this 50m uphill, then fork right on a lovely flat path. This undulates gently, circling to the right along the seaside slopes, passing through small woods and olive groves. At several points you have fine views across the Gulf. After going past a restored old STONE HOUSE ignore Route 3n off right for Barbazzano. Carry on along ROUTE 3, which becomes stony underfoot. It follows old drystone walls and dips through a hollow to arrive at ruined **Portesone** (138m; **2h40min**). This hamlet was abandoned by the inhabitants at the start of the 16th century

*Ligurian Sea*

*Between Serra and Portesone, with a backdrop of Lerici Bay*

following an epidemic of plague.

The direct route 3l from here down to Tellaro is uncomfortably stony, so it's best to keep straight ahead on Route 3 for a short while longer. You pass an old RUIN and ignore Routes 466 and 3h off right, to arrive at an old STONE HUT built under a rock face (155m). From here you enjoy a superb panoramic view across Tellaro to Palmaria Island. Turn back here and retrace your steps some 100m, then turn left down ROUTE 3h, a cobbled mule trail. This descends past steep drops to the bay and enters the tightly clustered centre of **Tellaro (3h)**. Ignore small Piazza Figoli on the right, go underneath an ARCH and continue to the left on VIA DELLA PACE. Behind a small CHURCH you emerge in a small PANORAMIC SQUARE above the foaming sea. Walk under another arch and go downhill on VIA SAN GIORGIO to SAN GIORGIO CHURCH, overlooking the idyllic tiny harbour bay. From BAR MARINA take the stepped pedestrian lane VIA PELLOSINI uphill to the LERICI ROAD (**3h10min**).

Instead of getting on the bus here you might extend the walk to a nice beach: Follow the road to Lerici for some 10 minutes, through the scattered houses of **Fiascherino**. Past RISTORANTE DELFINO, watch for a signpost '2 SPIAGGE', where a stepped footpath takes you down to **Sano di Traggiano** on the left. Turn right behind HOTEL SENATORE, to arrive at the far side of the spit of land. From the idyllic sandy beach of **Sano delle Stelle** you look out to the rocky cliffs of **Punta Mazzana** rising from the sea. Finally, from the mouth of a stream at the far end of the small crescent bay, take a flight of steps back up to the LERICI ROAD (**3h30min**); a BUS STOP is to the right.

## Walk 10: FROM TELLARO TO LERICI VIA AMEGLIA — ACROSS MONTEMARCELLO NATURE RESERVE

See photograph on page 53
Distance/time: 10km/6.2mi;
3h30min
Grade: easy-moderate; overall
ascent of 480m/1600ft and
descent of 520m/1700ft;
mainly easy underfoot; about
40min on small roads
Route-finding: fairly easy;
red/white waymarks with black
route numbers and signposts
throughout; from Tellaro to
Zanego Routes 3l and 3, from
there to Ameglia Route 2b,
then to Lerici Route 2
Equipment: as pages 12-13
Refreshments: bar in the
centre of Ameglia and in Serra
below the church square
Transport: 🚌 bus from Lerici
back to Tellaro (one per hour
on workdays, last departure
around 19.30; on Sundays five

buses in the afternoon
Map: as Walk 9, page 50
Longer walk: Circuit from
Tellaro. 12km/7.4mi; 4h;
moderate; overall ascent of
550m/1800ft and descent of
600m/1970ft). In Serra, at
house VIA GARIBALDI 8, turn left
on small VIA DELLA MONTANA
(◼ TELLARO, RED AND WHITE
WAYMARKS, ROUTE 464). This
descends through gardens, past
a FOUNTAIN on the left. Below
Serra you cross the LERICI–
MONTEMARCELLO ROAD. Carry
on along a cobbled mule trail.
Five minutes from the road it
meets ROUTE 3 rising from
Lerici (3h10min). Turn left
and follow the route of Walk 9
to Portesone. Turn right here
to retrace your outgoing route
downhill to Tellaro (4h).

To the southeast of La Spezia a small but striking mountain range, only 400 metres high, rises like a peninsula between the broad plain of the Magra River mouth and the Ligurian Sea. This thinly populated coastal area has been part of the Parco Regionale di Montemarcello-Magra since 1995, so it's protected from overdevelopment. This walk through the nature reserve follows old cobbled paths and trails across hills covered with small gardens, olive groves and typical Mediterranean macchia. All along the route you get extensive views across the Gulf of La Spezia and towards the steep marble cliffs of the Apuan Alps in Tuscany.

Start the walk in Tellaro
from the final BUS STOP in front
of ALBERGO DELLE ONDINE
(40m). Go back some 50m on
the main road towards Lerici.
Immediately behind the HOTEL
MIRAMARE CAR PARK turn right
uphill on the stepped footpath
VIA DELLA FONTE (◼ PORTESONE/
LERICI, RED AND WHITE WAY-
MARKS, ROUTE 3l). The trail
crosses a small road in under
five minutes, swings right
round the back of the highest

houses in Tellaro and reduces
to an old cobbled mule trail.
You climb through an olive
grove, stony underfoot, to the
ruins of Portesone (138m;
20min), a hamlet completely
abandoned during the 16th
century following an epidemic
of plague.
At the T-crossing behind the
ruins turn right (◼ MONTE-
MARCELLO/BOCCA DI MAGRA,
RED AND WHITE WAYMARKS,
ROUTE 3). The path contours

54

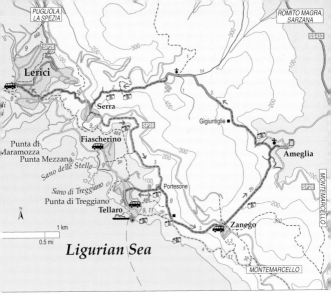

along the hillside, passing a RUIN, where Route 466 comes up right from Tellaro. Keep straight ahead, ignoring Route 3h from Tellaro coming in as well. Soon after you go past an old STONE HUT built under a rock face, where you enjoy excellent views down to Tellaro clustered round a ledge above the sea. From here the perfectly cobbled mule trail starts rising through a thin forest of holm oaks. Skirting the walls of scattered houses, you arrive at the hamlet of **Zanego** (235m; **50min**).

Cross the ROAD FROM LERICI TO MONTEMARCELLO and take the concrete trail descending to the left of an OPEN AIR ALTAR (⏴ AMEGLIA, RED AND WHITE WAYMARKS, ROUTE 2b). After 150m the concrete trail reduces to a pleasant earthen path. It winds its way steadily downhill along the northern flank of a green valley full of songbirds. Straight ahead, the limestone mountains of the Alpi Apuane rise steeply from the Magra Plain. After a short drop across an old landslide you descend

through olive trees and dip through a streambed, where you ignore a right turn. A few minutes later the path runs into a descending track. It swings left with views towards the ruin of the medieval castle in Ameglia.

At the upper edge of **Ameglia** you meet an old VILLA WITH A TOWER (HOUSE NUMBER 55/57). You want to take Route 2 for Serra/Lerici, which starts to the left of this building. But first walk straight ahead along the track, taking a short diversion of 10 minutes return, to pass the main CHURCH and visit Ameglia's small central SQUARE below the CASTLE RUINS (85m; **1h30min**; bar).

Go back to the villa with the tower and fork right on the ascending path (⏴ SERRA, RED AND WHITE WAYMARKS, ROUTE 2). It climbs steadily through a forest of chestnut and oak. Some five minutes from the villa it bends a little to the left via some steep wooden steps. At a fork keep left again but, 100m further on, turn sharp right, once more on wooden

55

steps. A few minutes later the views open up back towards Ameglia with the backdrop of the Alpi Apuane. The gradient lessens a little. A steady ascent along the wooded eastern slopes of the range takes you to an old drystone wall. Follow this uphill, to meet a track in front of the few old houses of **Gigiuntiglie**, today a nicely located rural B&B (**2h10min**).

Turn right on the track. After five minutes it becomes a small tarmac road rising gently along the edge of some meadows on the left. Go right at a fork, and at the following T-junction bear left, ignoring route 1V to Romito off right. Carry on uphill on the small road. Soon after crossing waymarked Route 1 it leads to a pass, where you meet a wider road (365m; **2h25min**). Follow this straight ahead downhill, past a HOUSE WITH A BELL-TOWER on your right.

Less than 100m further on, 30m behind a RED HOUSE on the left side of the road, take the path climbing the bank (ROUTE 2 WAYMARKS). After a short ascent you pass the gate of a big villa and then keep to the left of a lone house, to descend an old cobbled mule trail. This swings down left, to a track. Follow the track to the left for just 30m, to the ENTRANCE TO AN ESTATE, where you branch off right on a path. This runs through a dark forest following broken drystone walls and the few remains of a long-time abandoned HAMLET, today completely overgrown with vegetation. Leaving the wood, the views open out to reveal the bays and islands of the Gulf of La Spezia. After crossing a track, the cobbled

trail widens and descends across open terrain between walls, gardens and pines. You pass a HOUSE on the open hillside, beyond which a grassy path carries on downhill, with more far-reaching views over the tiled rooftops of Serra to the sea.

The path joins a small tarred road, which descends to the upper edge of **Serra**. Keep ahead on VIA GARIBALDI, which drops down through the village. At VIA GARIBALDI NUMBER 8 Route 464 to Tellaro forks off left. *(The Longer walk forks left here.)* Turn right on VIA COSTA, walking under an ARCH. Go across Serra's CHURCH SQUARE to the main road skirting the lower edge of the village (160m; **3h**).

Go 30m to the left, then turn right in front of BAR MIRO, to continue descending on VIA ZANELLI. It goes past the old SCHOOL on the left, bends right, and narrows to a tarred track. Ignore waymarked Route 462 off right; head left to some houses. Keep ahead, and go down a stepped foot-path. Within five minutes you meet the LERICI-TELLARO ROAD. Turn right for 50m; then, just past the turn-off for Maralunga, take another stepped path, (WAYMARKED ROUTE 3) down to PIAZZA GARIBALDI by **Lerici**'s harbour bay (**3h30min**).

## Walk 11: FROM TELLARO TO MONTEMARCELLO — VIEWS TO THE MARBLE MOUNTAINS

**See also photo pages 6-7**
**Distance/time:** 13km/8mi; 5h
**Grade:** moderate-strenuous, with an overall ascent of 780m/2560ft and descent of 570m/1870ft; between Montemarcello and Punta Bianca two steep, stony descents require attention, especially when the ground is wet
**Route-finding:** fairly easy; red/white waymarks with black route numbers and signposts throughout; from Tellaro Routes 3h, 4, 3g, 3, 1e and 1 up to Montemarcello; thereafter 3d to Punta Corvo; Routes 4 and 3 for the return to Montemarcello
**Equipment:** as pages 12-13; don't forget swimwear in summer (good beach en route)
**Refreshments:** three bars at Montemarcello
**Transport:** 🚌 bus from Montemarcello to Lerici (via Zanego; departs Mon-Sat at 14.10, 17.10, 18.10; *or* 15.10 bus from Montemarcello to Sarzana, change at Romito Magra for Lerici; then 🚌 from Lerici to Tellaro as Walk 10, page 54
**Map:** as Walk 9, page 50
**Alternative walk: Tellaro to Bocca di Magra.** 12km/7.4mi; 4h45min; moderate-strenuous, with an overall ascent of 680m/2230ft and descent of 700m/2300ft. In summer a small ferry plies along the coast between Bocca di Magra and Lerici. This can be used to return to the starting point, if you end the walk at Bocca di Magra instead of Montemarcello: at the 4.15min-point turn right on the descending trail for Bocca di Magra (ROUTE 3 AVG). It passes the entrance to SANTA CROCE convent.

Ignore the bend of a road on the left and go down the long flight of steps which emerges on a small beach at the wide MOUTH OF **river Magra**, busy with sailing and motor yachts. Turn left and go past another small beach and a concrete square to arrive at the YACHT HARBOUR. From here follow the tarmac road into the modest summer holiday village of **Bocca di Magra**. Following the shoreline promenade north you arrive at the FERRY QUAY (**4h45min**). To the left, 30m inland on VIA SAN FACON there's also a BUS STOP (tickets available at the Tabacchi at Via Fabbricotti 184). 🚢 Ferries run from Bocca di Magra to Lerici via Tellaro and San Terenzo from the end of May to the end of September 4-6 times per day; no departures in stormy weather; for timetables see www.navigazionefoce magra.it. There is also a 🚌 bus to Lerici at 14.32 and 15.32 (Mon-Sat) and another at 17.17 (Mon-Fri); in both cases change at Romito Magra.

*Punta Bianca*

This third walk in the Montemarcello Nature Park is full of variety. It leads into an unspoilt Mediterranean coastal landscape. You follow narrow panoramic footpaths and perfectly cobbled mule trails uphill to the silent hilltop village of Montemarcello. A steep descent leads from here down onto a secluded beach. As you circle round the southern end of the Montemarcello hills, the Alpi Apuane in Tuscany come into sight, forming an impressive backdrop of steep marble cliffs rising from the Magra Plain.

**Start the walk in Tellaro** from the final BUS STOP (40m). Go past ALBERGO DELLE ONDINE on VIA FIASCHERINO and cross PIAZZA FIGOLI to the entrance to the small historic TOWN CENTRE. At the end of Piazza Figoli, turn left on a small pedestrianised lane, VIA G MATTEOTTI (⁕ ZANEGO/MONTE-MARCELLO, RED AND WHITE WAYMARKS, ROUTE 3h). Climbing from the end of the village, this changes to a cobbled mule trail, after two minutes passing a view into a bay far below on the right. At the following junction, less than 10 minutes from the start, fork right on a smaller path, changing to waymarked ROUTE 4 (⁕ MONTEMARCELLO/BOCCA DI MAGRA).

Carry on five minutes slightly downhill along the steep seaside slope to another fork (**15min**). Turn left to start a long ascent, which initially rises over stony terraces. You soon pass an old STONE HOUSE surrounded by olive trees and ideally sited for good sea views. Behind the building head left uphill on natural stone steps. From the upper edge of the terraces the path swings right and levels off briefly. Passing between almost adjacent

*There are no sights in Tellaro; the village itself is the 'sight'!*

drystone walls, you enter the shade of a wood. The path bears left via some wooden steps, climbs steeply for five minutes, then descends through a dense forest — a sort of Mediterranean jungle — to the upper edge of a LANDSLIDE (**40min**). Here you are only around 100m in height above the sea, visible below.

The trail passes a RUIN on the right and starts going steeply uphill through a forest of pines and holm oaks. After a succession of hairpin bends

you come to a T-junction, where Routes 1 and 3 enter from the left (**1h**). Turn right, keeping to ROUTE 4. It skirts the lower end of a fenced grassy slope and continues round to the left, uphill. You arrive at a junction (*easily missed*), where Route 4 turns off sharply to the right. Park signboards here warn about possible rockfall on Route 4, so keep straight ahead on ROUTE 3g, still heading uphill. Some 10 minutes from the junction, a track coming from the nearby hamlet of Zanego is met (**1h20min**).

Turn right on this track to follow ROUTE 3 towards Montemarcello. The track rises gently under pines for five minutes. It levels out with the LERICI–MONTEMARCELLO ROAD on the left and a PANORAMIC GRASSY TERRACE on the right. Keep to the trail straight ahead. Some five minutes later

cross the MONTEMARCELLO ROAD. Now an old cobbled mule trail takes you across a hollow with a hump of cypresses. Once more you meet the tarmac road. Follow it only 100m towards Montemarcello, then fork left on a small woodland path (**1h40min**). Three minutes later, where Route 3 turns uphill to the right, keep to the path along the valley floor (▪ FOCE DI LIZZANO, ROUTE 1e).

After skirting a meadow, a short climb in the wood takes you up to the AMEGLIA–MONTEMARCELLO ROAD. Go 50m to the left and then take the path off to the right, running along the CEMETERY WALL on your left. At a Y-junction 100m past the cemetery, fork right (ROUTE 1 AVG). You rise along the wooded hillside on an old cobbled trail. Climbing up the bank you again join the AMEGLIA ROAD, which takes

you in three minutes to the BUS STOP at the northeastern edge of **Montemarcello**. Leave the road here: head left to enter the historical village centre via the small *MEDIEVAL TOWN GATE* by the *TRATTORIA DEI PIRON-CELLI (only open for dinner)*. Carry on straight ahead along a dark and narrow lane, then turn left in front of the main CHURCH. Past a bar and a grocer's shop, you emerge in the small central square, the *PIAZZA XIII DICEMBRE* (**2h05min**).

From here take the small *VIA CORVO* down to the right; this heads south out of the village. The small road swings a little to the right to meet the *MONTEMARCELLO–BOCCA DI MAGRA ROAD* next to the bar IL GIARDINO and the *TOURIST OFFICE (normally closed)*. Cross the road and descend on narrow *VIA DON CALISTO DEI MARCHI* (☛ *PUNTA CORVO, ROUTE 3d*). At the junction at *HOUSE NUMBER 28*, where Route 4c goes off left, bear right. The trail soon narrows to an earthen path, going gently downhill, past a *RUIN* and lined by drystone walls and brambles. About 10 minutes down from Montemarcello you come to a T-junction, where you meet *ROUTE 4* again. Follow it to the left. Some five minutes down you come to a shady *REST AREA WITH BENCHES* (**2h20min**).

From here we take a diversion of 40min return. Route 3d, forking off right behind the rest area, makes a rewarding detour to an unspoilt beach. You zigzag steeply downhill on a path stabilized by wooden planks, accompanied by the scent of pine and the roar of the foaming surf. At the end of the descent you step over some rocks onto the grey sand- and pebble beach **Spiaggia Punta Corvo,** a good place for a swim. But don't rely on being here alone during high summer, when quite a few visitors come by boat. Retrace your steps up to the rest area at the 2h20min-point (now **3h**) and turn right ( *PUNTA BIANCA, ROUTE 4*). A good five minutes later the narrow path traverses a field of boulders that have fallen down from a steep rock face. It then leads through a sombre forest of holm oaks growing on abandoned terraces. With a zigzag uphill you reach a junction, where Route 4c from Montemarcello joins from the left (**3h20min**, including the detour to Punta Corvo). Keep straight ahead on ROUTE 4. It goes slightly downhill past RUINS and old drystone walls. About 10 minutes from the junction with Route 4c, the trail drops down steeply, in some places stony underfoot. You enjoy fine sea views, but you must also take great care because of the sloping terrain. From the END OF THE DESCENT (**3h30min**) keep left. The path, now level, takes you within five minutes to a WORLD WAR II BUNKER. After another five minutes on a flat trail above the coast you meet a track (**3h45min**). A short detour downhill to the right on Route 3a leads to a nice picnic spot by the sea (15min return): the track bends down right, to a large RUIN. From here take the path to the left, which goes down to the sea. Beyond another BUNKER on the left you emerge on an area of flat rock below

the white cliffs of the **Punta Bianca** land tip. When the water is calm, this is a good swimming spot.

Again retrace your steps, this time to the 3h45min-point, and take the track heading uphill to the right ( *BOCCA DI MAGRA/MONTEMARCELLO, ROUTE 3*). Some 10 minutes later it widens to a tarred road, running level, with far-reaching views to the impressive mountain range of the Alpi Apuane. Down to the right the large convent of SANTA CROCE comes in into sight *(the convent isn't open to visitors)*. At the end of the convent's fenced-in gardens you come to the crossing of the ALTA VIA DEL GOLFO, way-marked as ROUTE 3 AVG (**4h15min**, both detours included).

Turn left uphill here for Montemarcello. *(But if you are heading for Bocca di Magra on the Alternative walk, bear right downhill.)* Route 3 follows an old cobbled mule trail past some villas on the right, where it becomes a gravel track. This soon meets the ROAD COMING UP FROM BOCCA DI MAGRA (**4h25min**). The old trail straight ahead is buried under a new embankment, so bear 30m to the right, and take a path climbing to the left. Within three minutes it rejoins the old cobbled trail, which ascends gently through a verdant valley. The trail gradually becomes a little steeper. You cross a track (**4h45min**), continue uphill between walls, and quickly arrive at the first houses of **Montemarcello.** Keep right at a junction and continue wandering along the eastern side of the village centre to the BUS STOP (**5h**).

# The little Cinque Terre

## from Levanto to Moneglia

*Lavaggiorosso*

**A** largely unspoilt coastal mountain landscape continues to the north of the Cinque Terre. There's no major road along the seashore, and the railway line is almost completely hidden in tunnels. Although the villages and towns of this area are not quite as picturesque as the 'five lands', some of them have quite a lot of Mediterranean flair. Levanto, Bonassola and Moneglia are particularly good places for a relaxing holiday. They have good beaches and are less crowded with tourists than the five famous villages further south. The surroundings of this 'little Cinque Terre' offer plenty of hiking opportunities in landscapes as beautiful as those on the crowded trails between Levanto and Portovenere. And the Cinque Terre proper are only some 10 to 30 minutes' train ride away.

**Levanto**, the northern gateway to the Cinque Terre,

is a lively little town of about 6500 inhabitants. It stretches along a crescent bay with a long sandy beach. It has little in the way of attractive outskirts, but a colourful old quarter with plenty of shops, bars and restaurants. Levanto dates from medieval times, its oldest parts lie by a hill at the eastern end of the centre. Here you find the 13th-century LOGGIA DEL COMUNE, the 800-year-old ruins of SAN GIORGIO CASTLE and CITY WALLS and the lovely gothic church of SANT'ANDREA. This has a characteristic dark green/white-striped façade and a beautiful rose-window; the interior holds some fine artwork. **Levanto Bay** is a popular surfing spot, as it has the biggest waves in all of Liguria. To the south the steep underwater cliffs of **Punta Mesco** are good for diving excursions.

Like Levanto, **Bonassola** has a good long beach framed by wooded hills and olive groves and an old town quarter with narrow alleyways. But with only about 1000 inhabitants, the village has a rather sleepy atmosphere. It's a good place for travellers seeking quiet and unspoilt nature. Its only sight is the parish church SANTA CATERINA with its rich baroque decoration.

**Framura** has an unusual shape. It consists of several picturesque hamlets, stacked one above the other on open slopes from sea level up to 300m. Of all the villages of the Riviera di Levante, Framura has best kept its original character. There are only a few touristic facilities and only small stony coves for swimming.

**Deiva Marina** is split in two: a sleepy small village inland gathered around a large baroque CHURCH and a more modern part on the coast. The latter has some hotels and a good beach, but is so unattractive architecturally that I wouldn't recommend a holiday there.

Neighbouring **Moneglia** is much nicer. It's a good destination for combining hiking, swimming and sight-seeing excursions. In atmosphere it's midway between lively Levanto and calm Bonassola. The friendly little town of about 2900 inhabitants has a well-preserved old centre made up of narrow alleyways lined with small shops and bars. The pleasant beach is protected by a mole, so the shallow stretch of water by the shore stays temptingly warm until October. Have a look inside black- and white-striped SAN GIORGIO CHURCH, which houses various pieces of art, like a wooden sculpture of Saint George and the dragon and a 16th-century painting by Luca Cambiaso, native of Moneglia.

## Getting about

Approximately every hour there's a **local or regional train** from La Spezia to Sestri Levante or even Genoa, stopping at Levanto, Bonassola, Framura, Deiva Marina, Moneglia and Riva Trigoso. But take care boarding a train: not all local/regional trains stop at all stations (except for Moneglia and Levanto). From Levanto there are about six **intercity trains** a day to Sestri Levante/Chiavari/Rapallo/Santa Margherita Ligure/Genoa/Milano and to La Spezia/Pisa.

There are hardly any **buses**. A few local lines connect the coastal towns with inland villages (for instance from Levanto to Lizza, recommended for Walk 12). Another line connects Framura railway station with the upper parts of the village (on workdays only).

## Walk planning

There are five walks in this book covering the 'little Cinque Terre', two of them are quite short and easy (Framura to Bonassola and Deiva Marina to Framura). The other three are a bit more demanding. All routes are less busy than those in the Cinque Terre proper.

**Out of area walks:** All the walks in this book are possible from Levanto, but Walks 19, 26 and 27 require early starts on the first intercity towards Genoa at about 7am. Moneglia has quite good train connections too, allowing day-trips as far as Lerici and Genoa. With good planning, the same is true for the other three villages in the area.

## Accommodation

The 'little Cinque Terre', especially **Levanto**, has become more and more popular as an alternative, less crowded starting point for exploring the Cinque Terre and the Riviera. There are several hotels, like old VILLA MARGHERITA\*\*\*, with its pleasant garden (www.villa margherita.net, from 130 €). Cheaper options, both good value for money, with small but well-equipped rooms, are VILLA GENTILE\*\* (www.villa gentile.com) and LOCANDA LA LOGGIA\*\* next to the medieval Loggia del Comune (from 70 €). There is also a YOUTH HOSTEL near the centre and the beach, which has a dormitory and some double rooms.

Ten minutes outside **Bonassola**, VILLA BELVE-DERE\*\*\* offers good views and good quality (www. bonassolahotelvillabelvedere.com, from 120 €). At

**Framura Anzo** there's the friendly *HOTEL AUGUSTA*** (www.hotelaugustaframura.com). **Moneglia** has some good but relatively expensive 3-star hotels. Pleasant *VILLA EDERA***, on the outskirts of the town, offers double rooms from 130 € (www.villaedera.com). Lower in price (and quality) is solid *GIAN MARIA*** in the centre (from 80 €, www.alberghogianmaria.it).

*Santa Margherita Ligure*

## Walk 12: FROM LIZZA TO BONASSOLA VIA MONTE ROSSOLA — IN THE CINQUE TERRE'S 'BACK YARD'

**See also photograph page 62**
**Distance/time:** 14km/8.7mi; 5h25min
**Grade:** moderate-strenuous, with an overall ascent of 700m/ 2300ft and descent of 860m/ 2820ft; good paths and trails
**Route-finding:** quite easy in spite of poor or *non-existent waymarking*
**Equipment:** as pages 12-13
**Refreshments:** bar/seasonal restaurant at Agriturismo La Rossola; bar/trattoria Lorella at Montaretto (good quality, reasonable prices, cl Mon)

**Transport:** 🚌 bus from Levanto to Lizza (on workdays at 7.22, 8.55, 10.45); it starts from the post office on Via Jacopo da Levanto in the town centre, tickets available next door in Café Salty Dog; for timetables see www.atcesercizio.it (line Levanto–Dosso–Brazzo). To return 🚆 local train Bonassola–Levanto, departing about every hour
**Map:** Edizioni del Magistero, Carta dei Sentieri 1:25,000, Sheet SP-41 Levanto, Framura, Deiva, Moneglia

On this long and varied walk you feel far away from the touristic coast. Following little-used paths and trails you soon forget the hustle and bustle of the nearby Cinque Terre. The route starts from a wooded green valley a short way inland from Levanto, where colourful small villages dot the hillside. A long initial climb takes you up onto barren Monte Rossola, a reddish-coloured isolated mountain rising more than 500 metres from the coast. From here — but also from many other places along the walk — you enjoy superb views down to the blue sea. So walk on a clear day!

**Start the walk** from BUS STOP at the southern end of **Lizza** (192m). Take the concrete path opposite towards the village centre. Turn right in front of the first houses and descend steps to a small SQUARE with a WATER TAP on the left. Bear right once more, to leave the village on a sealed track heading south. This joins a side-road which takes you uphill. Soon, some 250m to the south of Lizza, you meet the LEVANTO ROAD by which you came on the bus. Opposite, take a path to the right of a STONE BUILDING WITH TWO GREEN DOORS. The path turns left immediately, in front of a big fig tree. This grassy old mule trail climbs

along the upper edge of an olive grove, with a drystone wall on the right. About three minutes up from the road it becomes a little overgrown for some 50m, where it bends right into a shady oak woods. Entering the forest the trail becomes clear again. Continue uphill, past a collapsed old STONE HOUSE to a SECOND RUIN, where the beautiful village of Lavaggiorosso comes into sight. Here the path veers left, to leave the thick forest. You cross more open terrain with bush heather, until you meet an obvious CROSSING TRAIL (**35min**).
Follow this to the right (|▪ IL COLLETTO, RED AND WHITE WAYMARKS, ROUTE 19). It's a

steady uphill pull through small patches of pine and over shiny reddish rocks along the steep eastern slopes of Monte Rossola. Once you have gained the ridge, ignore the right turn for Lavaggiorosso. Some 100m further on you arrive at **Il Colletto**, a cross-roads on a saddle to the north of Monte Rossola (445m; **1h05min**).

From here we take a detour onto panoramic Monte Rossola by turning sharp left *(no markings)*. The path rises with far-off views along the open slopes. Down to the right Bonassola Bay comes into view. After a short steep climb the path levels out for a while. A last uphill stretch leads to the CROSS ON THE SUMMIT OF **Monte Rossola** (563m, **1h30min**). The panoramic view from here over the

*Around Lizza*

Ligurian coast is impressive: on very clear days it reaches across the sea to the snow-covered Piedmont Alps. Retrace your steps to the **Il Colletto** crossroads (**1h 50min**) and keep straight ahead on gently rising way-marked ROUTE 19 (which is fitted with some wooden planks for mountain bike jumping). At a fork four minutes up from Il Colletto, turn half-left (▪ PIAN PUN-TASCO, RED AND WHITE WAY-MARKS, ROUTE 28). A good five minutes later you pass AGRITU-RISMO LA ROSSOLA on the left (**2h**). Now the climbing becomes stiffer for a while. As the route swings left through a thin forest of pines the sea-shore comes into view. After veering back right, the path gradually levels off. Down to the left the village of Monta-

retto appears — we visit it later in the walk. After crossing a small oak wood, the trail widens out (**2h30min**). Keep ahead along the ridge and ignore a track coming up from the left. Just after passing some metal signs for 'S.S. LEVANTO/PIAN PUNTASCO' on the left (and facing the other way), turn left on a small path (655m, POOR RED-WHITE WAY-MARKING). This leads gently downhill to the south of **Monte Guaitarola**, sparsely forested with black pines. In 10 minutes the path meets the LEVANTO–CASTAGNOLA ROAD by signs denoting the villages of BONASSOLA AND FRAMURA (605m; **2h55min**).

Cross the road and continue straight ahead on a forest track for some 40m; then, just 5m before a fork in the track, turn left on a faint grassy trail (overgrown at first and *not way-marked*). Deeply rutted in places, it descends through a thin forest along the eastern slopes of **Monte Grumo**. Some 10 minutes down from the road you join a track. Follow this to the right for about 20 minutes at the south of rocky Monte Grumo. Soon views open out to the sea. Rising gently, you arrive at the saddle **Foce dei Gaggi**, where four walking routes meet (550m; **3h35min**).

From now on it's almost all downhill. Follow the woodland trail to the left of a bench, descending along the seaside slope. Some 250m further on it veers left and gradually reduces to a path, descending gently through a thick forest of conifers. About 20 minutes down from Foce dei Gaggi the trail, now stony underfoot, runs behind a prominent limestone rock, where the sea comes into view. From here the path descends onto a terrace, crosses a patch of wood and joins a tarmac track, which takes you down to a CEMETERY WALL. Bear right in front of the wall and walk under an ARCH into the small SQUARE of **Reggimonti** village (364m; **4h05min**). Visit its nearby little CHURCH, then take some steps descending from the square to the FRAMURA–LEVANTO ROAD. Cross this and continue straight ahead downhill to the little CHURCH in neighbouring **Montaretto** (286m; **4h15min**).

The inviting bar-trattoria LORELLA is behind the church, but for the ongoing trail turn left *in front* of the church, to leave the village on a concrete track. At a fork behind a last house, follow the earthen track to the left ( SAN GIORGIO). On a left-hand bend some 10 minutes down from Montaretto, fork right on a stepped path. It zigzags down into a secluded valley, where you cross a stream on a FOOT-BRIDGE (**4h30min**) — an idyllic spot, with water pouring down through a cleft with rock pools and dragonflies galore. From here the path continues a short way downhill over rocky ground, then ascends through a shady holm oak wood to a tarmac road. Some 250m uphill it skirts the upper edge of **San Giorgio** village (**4h40min**).

By the VILLAGE SIGN take the stepped lane downhill. Turn left at a T-junction, under an ARCH. Keep right behind the arch and right again in front of HOUSE NUMBER 21, to walk under another ARCH. Now, from the bottom of the village, a sealed footpath leads you down towards the sea via gardens and olive groves. You join a steeply descending lane and, 10 minutes' down from San Giorgio, you cross the BONASSOLA ROAD. On a right-hand bend 100m further down, turn left to the panoramic CHIESA DI SAN GIORGIO before continuing to the right on the main trail.

After 100m the trail crosses a stream on a FOOTBRIDGE (**5h**). Turn left at the fork after the bridge and pass a house, a RESTORED MILL. Continue down the cobbled mule trail, with the valley on the left. A good 10 minutes down from the bridge you join a road. Cross straight over another road and take VIA CANEPINE, a stepped footpath. Five minutes sees you down at **Bonassola**'s RAILWAY STATION (**5h25min**).

## Walk 13: FROM FRAMURA RAILWAY STATION TO BONASSOLA — GREEN FORESTS, BLUE SEA

**Distance/time:** 9km/5.6mi; 3h
**Grade:** easy-moderate; some short steep sections; overall ascent/descent 375m/1230ft
**Route-finding:** easy; except for the initial road section red/white waymarks throughout
**Equipment:** as pages 12-13
**Refreshments:** a grocer's shop and the good bar/restaurant Lorella at Montaretto (reason-

able prices, closed Mondays)
**Transport:** 🚂 local train to Framura and back from Bonassola (about one an hour)
**Map:** as Walk 12, page 66
**Shorter walk: Framura to Bonassola direct.** 7km/4.3mi; 2h15min; easy; overall ascent/descent of 260m/850ft. Do the walk but omit the detour at the 55min-point to Montaretto.

T his fairly short, but still very varied walk explores the unspoilt rocky seashore south of Framura. After an initial short section along a small road, you join a lovely old coastal path which contours the hillside above the coast. With some ups and downs you traverse pine and holm oak woods, enjoying fine views down into blue bays. A detour half way along leads to the tiny and friendly village of Montaretto, where the rural bar/restaurant is a very pleasant place to take a break.

**Start the walk** from **Framura** RAILWAY STATION by walking through the station TUNNEL. On the following left-hand bend in the road, take a flight of steps uphill, to join VIA LUIGI DUINI. Turn right and stay on this small tarmac road for 15 minutes; there's little traffic, and you have superb views down to the sea, where a Madonna stands on a rocky

outcrop, guarding Framura's tiny harbour. The road climbs to a group of houses, a HOLIDAY RESORT. Ignore a path off left signposted to 'Montaretto/Bonassola Stazione' and carry on to the end of the tarmac. Then take the ongoing path, which forks 30m further on at a place signposted 'VAN-DARECCA' (**20min**).

Turn left (⟋ SVA SALICE/BONASSOLA, RED AND WHITE WAYMARKS). For about five minutes the path rises steeply on rocky ground. It then looses height through holm oak woods. A good 10 minutes from Vandarecca, a ledge on the right offers a splendid panoramic view over the uninhabited rocky coastline. (*Take care* at the edge of these vertical cliffs!) Carry on downhill into a wooded valley, where a little stream is crossed by a small

SEASONAL WATERFALL (60m; **40min**). From there the path zigzags steeply uphill for 15 minutes, leaving the valley. Once out of the forest the path joins a track serving the farmhouse POGGIO DEL SALICE. Follow the track 100m uphill, to the entrance gate of HOUSE NUMBER 3 (165m; **55min**).

Waymarked path Route 691 for Bonassola forks off sharp right in front of this house. *(The Shorter walk heads sharp right here.)* Before taking Route 691, however, it's pleasant to make a diversion to Montaretto: keep straight ahead on the earthen track for another 50m.

*Ten minutes after Vandarecca you enjoy a splendid coastal panorama*

Then turn right on a small path rising between a RUIN on the left and a PINK HOUSE with agaves on the right (⏵ MONTARETTO, RED AND WHITE WAYMARKS). It's a short stiff climb with far-reaching views along the open hillside. Cross a track diagonally to the left (**1h 05min**), to traverse a patch of woodland, climbing more gently. At an old wall-like OUTDOOR ALTAR you meet a tarmac track. This leads uphill past a grocer's shop (*alimentari*) to the CHURCH in the centre of **Montaretto** (286m; **1h20min**).

From Montaretto retrace your steps to the 55MIN-POINT (**1h40min**) and take the path to the left (⏵ BONASSOLA, RED AND WHITE WAYMARKS, ROUTE 691). It runs level along the upper edge of a vineyard, then enters a forest of holm oaks, where it bends to the right and crosses a small stream. After a short rise, it descends steadily to a track coming up from the right (**2h05min**). Follow this track uphill for three minutes, to a CROSSROADS ON A SADDLE. Turn right and, at the fork 20m further on, take the broad track rising to the left (⏵ STRADA PEDONALE SALTO DELLA LEPRE). At the highest point in the track, in front of a BARRIER (**2h15min**), turn left on a path. It soon starts descending through a sparse pine forest towards the sea. At a junction, keep straight ahead on the path — to where it ends 100m further on. This is **Salto della Lepre** (**2h30min**), a viewpoint on open hillside from where the whole coast from Genoa to the Punta

Mesco promontory of Levante comes into view.

Go back 100m to the junction and turn right (⏵ BONASSOLA). The path crosses a sweet-scented pine forest and runs above an estate with cypresses. Ignore a left turn signposted for Luca; keep straight ahead. The path swings left and contours along the hillside above Bonassola Bay. After a short steep descent between fences it meets a track (**2h45min**). Follow the track to the right. It veers left and joins a small road. Turn right here then, after about 30m, you come to the start of a small stepped lane. Follow this downhill to a small CHURCH overlooking **Bonassola Beach**. To get to the railway station 250m away, turn left and walk under the ARCHES of the disused old railway line. Go past SANTA CATARINA church on the left and follow the valley road, with the old centre of **Bonassola** on your right, to the RAILWAY STATION (**3h**).

*Near Salice (Walk 13 and Longer walk 14)*

## Walk 14: FROM DEIVA MARINA TO FRAMURA BEACH — THROUGH FRAMURA NATURE PARK

**Distance/time:** 9km/5.6mi; 3h
**Grade:** easy-moderate, with an overall ascent/descent of 350m/1150ft. Start early on warm sunny days, as the initial steep climb offers little shade
**Route-finding:** quite easy in spite of poor waymarking
**Equipment:** as pages 12-13
**Refreshments:** trattoria at the agriturismo Foce del Prato (good value); bars at Costa by the main road behind the defense tower, in the centre of Setta and, during the summer season, at Anzo harbour
**Transport:** 🚃 local train from Framura to Deiva Marina and back (about every hour)
**Map:** as Walk 12, page 66
**Longer walk:** Deiva Marina –Framura–Bonassola. 15km/ 9.3mi; 4h30min; moderate, with an overall ascent/descent of about 550m/1800ft. At the 2h25min-point keep straight ahead on the tarmac road *VIA LUIGI DUINI*. Follow *WALK 13* to **Bonassola** without diverting to Montaretto.

Some ten years ago the Monte Serro coastal mountain range between Deiva Marina and Framura was designated a nature reserve. This walk gives a good overview of the different landscapes of the small Parco Naturale di Framura. It starts with a panoramic but strenuous climb across the sun-exposed coastal slope, clothed in typical Mediterranean macchia. Later the going is more comfortable, as you contour the cooler northern side of the hills in the shade of sweet chestnuts, oaks and pines. Descending back to the sea, you pass the colourful hamlets of Framura. The walk ends at a small pebble beach good for a swim in clear waters.

*Villa at Framura Anzo*

**Start the walk** from **Deiva Marina** RAILWAY STATION. Walk 250m along the road parallel to the river, heading towards the sea. Cross the river on a modern bridge. Turn left on the opposite side, to go past HOTEL RIVIERA. Turn right before the big RAILWAY BRIDGE and follow a side road sign-posted for a camp ground. About 30m after a right-hand bend, turn off left (**10min**) on a path to the foothills (▪ CASE SERRO, FRAMURA, BONASSOLA; SPORADIC BLUE DOTS).
From here a stiff ascent begins. The path zigzags uphill through typical Mediterranean macchia — black pines,

strawberry bushes and tree heather. After 20 minutes' climbing, having rounded a small ROCKY AREA, keep left and ascend an eroded scree slope. Looking back you have fine sea views. Some 10 minutes later you cross a shady patch of wood and the gradient lessens. The path circles to the right through ferns growing beneath pine trees. After passing a LONE HOUSE on the right, it joins a track at the crossroads of **Case Serro** (300m; **1h**).
A few metres to the right there are fine views over the coast, but for the ongoing route take the path to the far left (▪ FOCE DEL PRATO/COSTA, FAINT RED AND WHITE WAYMARKS, ROUTE 651). At first there are also some WHITE ARROWS guiding you along this lovely path, easy underfoot, as you contour along the wooded northern slopes of the **Monte Serro** range, which rises to 421m. In places the view opens inland onto small villages lying in sparsely settled mountainous

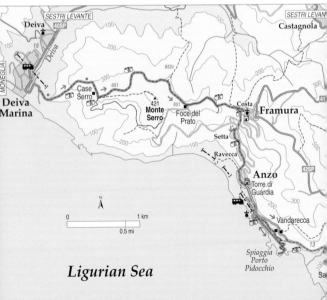

woodland. Ignore waymarked Route 652c off left for Case Vigo (**1h25min**). The path then swings round to the right, crosses the low saddle **Foce del Prato** (320m), then widens out a little. Some five minutes later you arrive at the AGRITU-RISMO/TRATTORIA FOCE DEL PRATO (325m; **1h40min**). Walk to the left of the group of houses on a track running along the inland side of the ridge *(no waymarks)*. At the end of a short steep descent the track reduces to a path. It leads to the already-visible village of **Costa**, the uppermost part of Framura. Bear right by the first houses, to emerge in a small SQUARE WITH BENCHES offering good sea views.

Your ongoing route down to the coast starts opposite HOUSE NUMBER 53, but first take a short detour along the ascending lane straight ahead, to a 9th-century DEFENSE TOWER (304m; **1h55min**).

Go back to house 53 and take a concrete footpath downhill. You twice cross the ROAD WHICH CONNECTS COSTA WITH FRAMURA RAILWAY STATION. You enter the colourful agglomeration of **Setta** on a small lane. At a T-junction in the village, turn left under an ARCH. Cross the small PIAZZA with an inviting bar on your left (160m; **2h10min**). Then, leaving Setta, turn right behind a rest area with benches. A small road takes you downhill (⚑ RAVECCA, ANZO). After 50m it reduces to a stepped path. Five minutes down from Setta you go through the hamlet of **Ravecca** on a narrow lane. Then, just before joining the station road, turn right downhill on a flight of steps (⚑ SPIAGGIA TORSEI, STAZIONE).

At the end of the steps keep left to enter **Anzo**, a tranquil small village with some large uninhabited villas, harking back to better times. Ignore a right turn for *'stazione'* and walk under the ARCH AT HOUSE NUMBER 16. Passing the medieval TORRE DI GUARDIA on the left you meet the station road. Follow this quiet road downhill for some five minutes. Then (**2h25min**), on a sharp right-hand bend, turn left on smaller VIA LUIGI DUINI (⚑ VANDARECCA).

Some 50m further on a flight of steps leads back down to the station road. But keep to the road three more minutes: below a villa with a tower take a cobbled footpath with rusty railings going off right (⚑ SPIAGGIA PORTOPIDOCCHIO). *(But for the Longer walk to Bonassola, stay on the road.)* The lovely path descends five minutes with fine sea views through pines and mediter-ranean scrub. At a signpost indicating the closure of a first flight of steps to the shore, the route climbs a little to the left, crosses a promontory and then winds its way down to the sea. Turning right in front of a lone house, you step onto the small shady pebble beach of **Portopidocchio Bay** (**2h45min**).

From the beach follow a path on the right uphill for three minutes, to meet a new cycle track (built over the former coastal railway line). Follow this to the left through an illuminated tunnel about 400m long. At the end take the metal staircase down into **Framura**'s small harbour, sheltered by a small rocky peninsula with a statue of the Madonna. A narrow road takes you under the new railway line and through a short tunnel, to the RAILWAY STATION (**3h**).

## Walk 15: FROM MONEGLIA TO DEIVA MARINA VIA MONTE INCISA — MARE E MONTI

**Distance/time:** 12km/7.4mi; 4h30min

**Grade:** moderate, with an overall ascent/descent of about 580m/1900ft; long, but not very steep initial climb; the descent path from Monte Telegrafo is stony and rutted in places for about half an hour

**Route-finding:** relatively easy; waymarks throughout

**Equipment:** as pages 12-13

**Refreshments:** none en route

**Transport:** 🚆 local train from Deiva Marina to Moneglia

**Map:** as Walk 12, page 66

**Shorter walk: Moneglia to Deiva.** 8km/5mi; 2h55min; easy-moderate. Omit the detour for Monte Incisa from the 1h50min-point.

**Alternative walk: Moneglia–Monte Incisa circuit.** 11km/6.8mi; 4h15min; moderate (ascent/descent as the main walk). Follow the main walk to **Monte Incisa** (514m; **2h 40min**), then retrace your steps to the SADDLE AT THE 2H20MIN-POINT (**3h**). At the fork here

leave your outgoing trail and take the small path to the right (*no waymarks*). It contours along the steep northwestern slopes of **Monte Telegrafo**. Descending through a forest you pass a STONE HUT, then join a wider trail (which ends at a gate 50m to the left). Follow this trail downhill to the right, with good views to Lemeglio. In **Lemeglio** village take the main footpath, descending past the CHURCH to the end of the tarmac ROAD FROM MONEGLIA (**3h35min**). From the BUS STOP here a stepped footpath takes you downhill (*RED SQUARE WAY-MARKS*). At Ristorante Ruota it rejoins the road. Follow this for about 10 minutes, ignoring a side-road off left. On a right-hand bend, take a concrete footpath descending straight ahead. At the eastern edge of **Moneglia** centre, near SANTA CROCE, rejoin your outgoing route and head back to the RAILWAY STATION (**4h15min**).

The long ridge of Monte Incisa, rising to 500m, drops almost vertically down to the coast between Moneglia and Deiva Marina — thus preventing easy road-building and development of the area. With a long ascent past the lovely little village of Lemeglio, you climb to the top of this uninhabited ridge, where the path winds its way through broom, strawberry bushes, heather and small holm oaks. The low and sparse Mediterranean vegetation up here allows superb views down into Moneglia Bay. Your final destination after the long descent back down to the sea is Deiva Marina, with a lovely old kernel and a holiday resort by the sea with a good beach but rather unattractive buildings.

**Start the walk** from **Moneglia** RAILWAY STATION. Walk 200m downhill on the station road and turn right on a footpath (⚑ ABADDIA SAN GIORGIO). It runs under an ARCH and past a row of houses to black- and white-striped SAN GIORGIO church. Take VIA ROMA diagonally to the left, to cross the valley road and continue ahead on VIA VITTORIA EMANUELE

76

*View from Monte Incisa into Moneglia Bay*

through the old town centre. Pass the large baroque church of SANTA CROCE on the left and go under the RAILWAY BRIDGE, turning left. Continue 30m on VIA LIBERAZIONE (the SP55) and cross the **Bisagno River** on a footbridge. Continue parallel to the river on the left, cross the ROAD FOR LEMEGLIO and a CAR PARK (**15min**). At its far end keep right, to join an old mule trail, VIA PER LITTORNO (☞ LITTORNO 1.30, BLUE WAYMARKS).

You cross the river on an old stone BRIDGE, to continue along the right bank. Some 150m further on the path bears right and rises away from the river. It crosses a SIDE STREAM (**25min**) and forks. Turn right, to ascend through a deciduous forest. After passing a RUIN, the path veers right to a small road. Turn left and go past the row of houses on the right, which make up **Littorno** (195m; **50min**).

About 20m before a RED CHAPEL, turn right behind the highest house in the hamlet (☞ LEMEGLIO, NO WAYMARKS). Descend a small, initially stony path to the left of an olive plantation into a damp forest and continue with short ups and downs on a somewhat uncomfortable trail (*note: the wooden railings here might be rotten!*).

A good five minutes from Littorno the path gradually improves and runs almost level through a sweet chestnut wood. At the foot of a steep slope planted with olive tree it swings right and rises steeply, with far-off views to the inland mountains. Once past a GATE turn left uphill. The village of Lemeglio with its

77

black- and white-striped church comes into sight. Follow a small path rising along the upper edge of an open slope, which allows far-reaching views down into Moneglia Bay. From the end of the climb a track leads into the village of **Lemeglio** (205m; **1h20min**).

Turn left at a T-junction (☛ *DEIVA, S NICOLAO, MEZZEMA, RED SQUARE WAYMARKS, THEN BLUE DOTS*). Leave the village to the east on an initially flat mule trail above a vineyard. Looking back, you have a good view of little Lemeglio. The trail soon enters a shady forest of holm oaks, where it starts to climb steeply over rocky ground. It levels out, swings left and passes a BENCH BESIDE AN IRON CROSS. With good sea views, continue along the open macchia-covered hillside until you come to a junction (295m; **1h50min**).

Your ongoing trail for Deiva goes off right, but for the moment take a detour onto panoramic Monte Incisa by turning left. Turn left again at the next fork only 30m away (☛ *MONTE TELEGRAFO, RED SQUARE WAYMARKS*). A stony, sometimes eroded path, winds its way uphill along the barren coastal slope. The steep ascent ends at a WOODEN CROSS on **Monte Telegrafo** (443m, **2h15min**). Continue straight ahead on a well-worn path following the ridge to the north. A short descent takes you to a SADDLE (430m; **2h 25min**). Here a small path joins from the left *(used on the Alternative walk circuit)*. Keep straight ahead and climb five more minutes. Some short undulations take you along the macchia-clad panoramic

summit ridge. At a rocky ledge on the left you reach the highest point of **Monte Incisa** (514m; **2h45min**).

Retrace your outward route back to the junction at the 1H50MIN-POINT (now **3h 25min**), where you turn left (☛ *DEIVA, BLUE DOT WAY-MARKS*). A well-worn path, sometimes deeply rutted, leads downhill towards the sea. It becomes easier underfoot when you enter a scented pine forest. Finally, circling to the left, you arrive at the CASTAG-NOLE FARMHOUSE (205m; **3h45min**).

Follow an earthen track to the left; it runs along the upper edge of an olive-growing area. A good five minutes from Castagnole it bends right and acquires a concrete surface. Dropping steeply for some 15 minutes you arrive at the first houses of **Deiva**. You cross a wide road and follow a narrow lane opposite into the small historic centre with the PIAZZA COLOMBO (**4h10min**). The large baroque village CHURCH stands on the left some 50m further on. But you turn right at Piazza Colombo, on a lane leading to the main road. Follow the pavement parallel to **Deiva River** to reach the RAILWAY STATION at **Deiva Marina** (**4h20min**). The beach is 250m away.

## Walk 16: FROM RIVA TRIGOSO TO MONEGLIA — MACCHIA TRAILS ABOVE THE SEA

**Distance/time:** 10km/6.2mi; 3h20min

**Grade:** easy-moderate, with an overall ascent/descent of around 400m/1300ft; little shade, so start out early in hot weather

**Route-finding:** fairly easy, since you're walking across open countryside, but waymarks are rare and faint

**Equipment:** as pages 12-13

**Refreshments:** none en route

**Transport:** 🚍 local train from Moneglia to Riva Trigoso (there are around 14 a day). *Note that not all local trains stop at Riva Trigoso!*

**Map:** Carta dei Sentieri, Sheet 40 Lavagna–Sestri–Moneglia–Framura (1:25,000, Federazione Italiana Escursionismo F.I.E., 6 €)

*On the trail*

In 2004 a disastrous brush fire destroyed the vast pine forests on the slopes of the uninhabited coast southeast of Riva Trigoso. This meant that the old coastal trail from there to Moneglia was transformed into a perfect panoramic walk. All along the route you enjoy fine views over bays and mountain ridges dipping into the sea. And with each passing year the damage created by the fire is less visible. The Mediterranean macchia is regaining ground, so that in spring and early summer the blooms of the broom, bush heather and cistus paint bright colours across the dark-green hillsides.

*Ligurian Sea*

**Start the walk** from **Riva Trigoso** RAILWAY STATION. Follow the road parallel to the rail lines 300m to the east, cross under the railway line and go past the wall of the CEMETERY. At its end take the small tarmac road rising to the left (⏴ PUNTA BAFFE, RARE WAYMARKS: TWO RED CIRCLES). The road bends left 100m further on, after which you turn right on a track (initially tarred). With far-reaching views inland to the Apennines, the track steadily gains height as it winds over treeless hills, where the ravages of the big brush fire are still visible. After 25 minutes' climbing, the track levels out and the sea comes into view. Some five minutes later the track reduces to a path, which soon starts rising steeply over rocky ground. At the end of the ascent you come to a Y-fork, where you bear right. Within five minutes you arrive at a ledge and the ruins of the TORRE PUNTA BAFFE (262m; **1h05min**). This medieval watchtower was part of a defensive system against pirates and Saracen raids. From here the views stretch south over bays and ridges to the steep promontory of Punta Mesco near Levanto.

Turn sharp left in front of the ruin and take a path climbing north along the eastern hillside (⏴ MONTE MONEGLIA). Another path joins from the left and the trail levels out, crossing a panoramic open ridge. After another short way uphill you come to a CROSSROADS BY A WOODEN BENCH (320m; **1h30min**).

Turn right here (⏴ MONEGLIA, RARE WAYMARKS: TWO RED CROSSES). The path rises for 10 more minutes, gaining about 50m in height. Then it contours along the seaward-facing hillside with short undulations. The barren slopes assure you of constant good views. Swinging left, the trail dips through a shady depression, where you cross a STREAM (**1h50min**) which carries a lot of water in spring but runs dry in summer. From here the path climbs steeply for three minutes, then swings right across another STREAMBED (**2h20min**). After passing through a small forest of young pines you come to a fork (310m; **2h40min**). Some 100m to the right there's a picnic place with a fine view deep down into Moneglia Bay. But for Moneglia itself, turn left (⏴ MONEGLIA, WAYMARKS: TWO RED CROSSES PLUS STRIPE WITH DOT).

The path soon starts descending towards Moneglia Bay. It goes past a fence on the right, traverses a shady forest of holm oaks and comes to a crossing. Bearing right through a dark defile, you meet a small road coming from a PINK HOUSE on the left (**3h**). Follow the road downhill for about 10 minutes, until it bends left and goes past HOTEL MONDIAL to HOTEL VILLA EDERA. In front of Villa Edera's car park, take the old cobbled mule trail off to the right. It descends alongside the walls of a CASTLE-LIKE 19TH-CENTURY VILLA, falling to ruins. Beyond an ARCH, turn left to **Moneglia**'s black- and white-striped CHIESA SAN GIORGIO. Continuing half-right along VIA ROMA you would reach the old TOWN CENTRE and BEACH in five minutes. Turning left in front of the church and going under an arch, you join the road up to the nearby RAILWAY STATION (**3h30min**).

# The Tigullio Gulf

## Lively towns, barren ridges

*Sestri Levante*

The Tigullio Gulf extends from the Portofino Peninsula in the north to the Punta Manara promontory of Sestri Levante in the south. It covers a densely populated coastal area about 25 kilometres in length. In some places the mountain ranges of the Apennines have left enough room for sizeable urban development. That's why in each of the four main towns — Sestri Levante, Chiavari, Rapallo and Santa Margherita Ligure — you will find vivid and colourful historic centres sitting almost side-by-side with ugly over-development. But the backdrop is wonderful: sparsely inhabited green mountain ranges rising to 600-800m — which offer amazingly good hiking opportunities — as well as the high Apennines of the Aveto Nature Reserve further inland, an isolated mountain area rising up to 1800 metres.

The picturesque old town of **Sestri Levante** stretches across a small peninsula between two bays, BAIA DEL FAVOLE and BAIA DEL SILENZIO. A typical lively Ligurian *carrugio*, VIA XXV APRILE, runs through the historic centre. This small pedestrian lane is lined by some attractive buildings decorated with slate reliefs and *trompe l'oeil* façades. Exquisite shops offer all sorts of tasty morsels. Via XXV Aprile ends near Sestri Levante's main 'sight': scenic Baia del Silenzio. Its crescent-shaped sandy beach is lined by colourful Genoese façades mirrored in the shallow waters. A little medieval church, SAN NICOLO, and a 13th-century tower, TORRE GUGLIELMO MARCONI (used by the famous Italian physicist in 1932-34 for his experiments on wireless telegraphy), stand at the highest point of the peninsula.

At first sight **Chiavari** seems to be a fairly unattractive town. It sits in the middle of a plain full of uninspiring modern architecture. But the old centre with its cosy squares, old archways, medieval and baroque houses and its 19th-century palaces paints a completely different picture. Chiavari is a pleasant 'everyday' Italian town and marketplace with original small shops, cafés and restaurants.

Chiavari's CATHEDRAL, with its big temple-like 17th-century front, is just by the station. Almost next to it you will find the main PIAZZA MAZZINI with the PALAZZO DI GIUSTIZIA, rebuilt in 1886 in medieval style, and the 17th-century PALAZZO TORRIGLIA (at Piazza Mazzini 1). Every morning except Sundays a colourful outdoor fruit, fish and vegetable MARKET is held in this square. The main shopping street, VIA MARTIRI DELLA LIBERA-ZIONE, crosses the northern side of the square: it's been the lively centre of the city since the 14th century.

The railway line separates the historic centre from the seashore, where you find an average pebble beach extending in a straight line up to Cavi. The BASILICA SAN SALVATORE DEI FIESCHI, some five kilometres out of town, to the north of Lavagna, is one of the most beautiful and best-preserved medieval churches in Liguria. Finally, Chiavari is also the gateway to the Aveto Nature Reserve of the high Apennines.

In the 19th and early 20th centuries **Rapallo** was a very exclusive seaside resort. But after World War II a lot of the city's original buildings were torn down and rebuilt in a more modern style, so that Rapallo lost its elegant atmosphere. But some old narrow alleyways in the inner city still have some charm. There is a lively local morning MARKET from Monday to Saturday in the small central PIAZZA VENEZIA. The main street along the coast, LUNGOMARE V VENETO, has a typical Mediterranean flair — with palm trees, hotels and the CHIOSCO DELLA BANDA CITTADINA. On the ceiling of this old pavillion there are paintings of well-known composers, including Verdi, Berlioz, Beethoven and Mozart. A small CASTLE stands in front of the shore, built in the 16th century as a defence against Saracen raids.

From Rapallo Liguria's only FUNIVIA (CABLE CAR) climbs 600 metres to the SANCTUARY OF MADONNA DI MONTALLEGRO. This large white church was built in the 16th century, then rebuilt in the 18th and 19th centuries in baroque and neo-gothic style. The Madonna of Montallegro is the local patron saint of the seafarers. Votive tablets of sailors saved from shipwreck decorate the walls inside the church.

Like Rapallo, neighbouring **Santa Margherita Ligure** (shown on page 65) was transformed in the 19th century from a simple fishing village into one of the most fashionable resorts on the Riviera, attracting famous writers like Hemingway, Pound and Nietzsche. But unlike Rapallo, it has somehow kept its aristocratic allure even today. The town is still dominated by the luxurious 19th-century villas lining the coast, and the crescent harbour bay is full of luxury yachts of all sizes. The main church, SANTA MARGHERITA D'ANTIOCHIA in the centre of the old town, is splendidly opulent with gold and crystal. And don't miss the 16th-century VILLA DURAZZO: from the park with its exotic plants and statues you have a magnificent view across the bay.

## Getting about

There is a **local or regional train** from Sestri Levante to Lavagna, Chiavari, Rapallo, Santa Margherita Ligure, Camogli, Recco and Genoa: this runs every 30-60 minutes on workdays, about hourly on Sundays. There's approximately one departure an hour to the south for the Cinque Terre and La Spezia. **Intercity trains** from Livorno/Pisa to Genoa and Milan via La Spezia, Monterosso and Levanto stop at Sestri Levante (9 a day), Chiavari (9 a day), Rapallo (9 a day), Santa

Margherita Ligure (5 a day). Fast **Frecciabianca** trains from Genoa to Rome via La Spezia/Pisa stop at Chiavari and Rapallo three times a day.

There are frequent **buses** along the coastal road (Via Aurelia) from Riva Ligure to Chiavari via Sestri Levante, Cavi and Lavagna (about every 40 minutes) and from Chiavari to Rapallo via Zoagli (hourly); for timetables see www.atpesercizio.it.

## Walk planning

The five walks in this area differ considerably with regard to grade and length. Walks 17 (Riva to Sestri Levante) and 20 (Montallegro to Zoagli) are quite easy and short; Walks 18 (circuit from Sestri Levante) and 19 (Belvedere to Gramizza) are only demanding because of their length; Walk 21 (Ruta to Monte Manico del Lume), on the other hand, is only suitable for experienced hikers. But I have suggested shorter and easier variations for both Walks 18 and 21.

**Out of area walks:** Since the train connections from Rapallo, Chiavari, Sestri Levante, and to a lesser degree from Santa Margherita Ligure, are so good, *all* the walks in this book are possible as day-trips — although the walks starting to the south of Manarola demand quite long bus and train journeys.

## Accommodation

**Sestri Levante** has some expensive high-class hotels like Villa Balbi or the Helvetia overlooking the Bay of Silence. Cheaper accommodation is available at the HOTEL MARINA** (www.marinahotel.it, about 80 €) or simple old town HOTEL SAN PIETRO* (www.albergo ristorantesanpietro.it, from 65 €). In **Chiavari** old-established and calm HOTEL MONTEROSA*** in the old town is a good choice (www.hotelmonterosa.it, from 115 €). Simple MIRAMARE** is a budget hotel on the sea-side promenade (www.albergoristorantemiramare.it, from 60 €). Friendly ALBERGO BANDONI in the centre of **Rapallo** is very old-fashioned, but also inexpensive with double rooms ranging from 50 to 75 €; some even have sea views. **Santa Margherita Ligure** has mainly expensive high-class accommodation; one of the few cheaper options is HOTEL VILLA ANITA** (www.hotel viallaanita.com, about 100 €).

## *Walk 17:* FROM RIVA TRIGOSO T… LEVANTE — ABOVE THE BAY OF SI…

**See photograph on page 81**
**Distance/time:** 7km/4.3mi; 2h10min
**Grade:** easy, with an overall ascent/descent of 230m/755ft; you must be sure-footed for the short detour onto the narrow ridge of Punta Manara
**Route-finding:** for the first half hour up to Villa Ginestra you have to take care, as there are no waymarks; otherwise easy. Waymarks: two hollow red triangles a… Villa Ginestra to … Manara, red square… re to Sestri Levante
**Equipment:** as pages 12-13
**Refreshments:** none en route
**Transport:** 🚌 hourly bus from Sestri Levante to Riva Trigoso; it stops in Sestri Levante on Piazza Italia, where the station road Viale Roma joins the main Viale Mazzini
**Map:** as walk 16, page 79

This relatively short walk follows mostly well maintained coastal paths, easy underfoot, through pine wood and Mediterranean macchia. From the small coastal town of Riva Trigoso it climbs onto Punta Manara, a rocky promontory jutting far out into the sea. From the edge of the steep cliffs you enjoy fine views over the bays and coastal ranges between Monte Portofino in the north and Punta Mesco in the south. On the way down from here to Sestri Levante, a small peninsula, embracing the calm little 'Bay of Silence' (Baia del Silenzio), paints an attractive picture.

**Start the walk** by alighting at the terminus of the bus line in **Riva Trivoso**'s town centre, on the far side of the bridge across the small river **Petronio**. Turn back, cross the BRIDGE and walk west on *VIA GIACOMO BALBI* running parallel to the shore. After 200m bend right and follow the main road, *VIA M VATTONA*, inland. Just behind HOUSE NUMBER 160 head left on the paved walkway *VIA VILLA ROCCHE*. Within three minutes this rises via steps into the hamlet of **Villa Rocche** (**10min**).

A path starts here, at the left side of the buildings. It rises steeply in the shade of trees. Keep left at a fork. Some five minutes above Villa Rocche the gradient lessens. At the following T-junction a sign *'SENTIERO PERICOLOSO'* ('dangerous path') warns you against turning left, so go right (SMALL, SINGLE RED DOT WAYMARK). You walk a short way on the flat alongside an olive grove, climb some steps, and cross another olive grove, to come into the hamlet of **Villa Ginestra**. At HOUSE NUMBER 33, opposite a B&B, you join a small road (**30min**).

Follow this 100m uphill, then leave the tarmac in front of a PYLON, taking the path to the right (⚑ PUNTA MANARA, TWO HOLLOW RED TRIANGLES). Around 50m further on bear left, ignoring the path ahead signposted for Sestri Levante. After three minutes' steep climbing, the trail levels out and runs through scrub high above the coast, with views down to Riva's bay with its shipyard. When another path

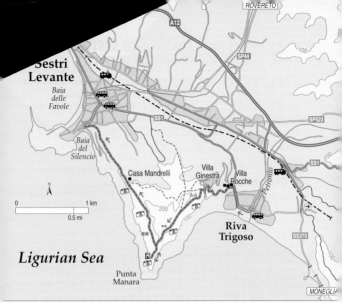

joins from the right, keep to the trail straight ahead (WAY-MARKS CHANGE TO RED DOTS). In less than five minutes you come to a rest area with a wooden BENCH (205m). After another five minutes the path starts to descend over rocky ground to a fork on a SADDLE (**1h05min**).

The trail sharp right goes off to Sestri Levante. But before you follow this, take a short detour onto the Punta Manara peninsula by taking the path to the left. It goes past a small building 50m ahead and rises by a flight of steps to a RUINED TOWER. From here a small, exposed path extends for about 100m along the narrow rocky ridge of panoramic **Punta Manara** (166m).

Retrace your steps to the SADDLE (**1h15min**) and keep left (⊩ SESTRI LEVANTE, RED SQUARES). A well-worn trail runs nearly level along the western hillside, where the colourful crescent-shaped bay of Sestri Levante comes into view. Sometimes running over sandy ground, the path winds

its way through low macchia and sparse black pine woods. About 20 minutes from the saddle it starts to descend over stony ground, offering far-reaching views. Keeping to the path straight ahead you come down to CASA MANDRELLI, an isolated little hillside farm-house in a splendid panoramic position (**1h45min**).

Pass to the left of this private property and continue along the wooded ridge, keeping to the same direction. Some five minutes past Casa Mandrelli the path starts to descend between old walls. At the first houses of **Sestri Levante** it changes to a sealed stepped walkway, which emerges on a small lane, VICO BOTTONE. You go under an ARCH and join VIA XXV APRILE, the main pedestrian alleyway traversing the old town. About 150m to the left the beautiful **Baia del Silenzio** opens up (**2h10min**). But heading right, away from the bay, Via XXV Aprile takes you back to the BUS STOP on PIAZZA ITALIA near the railway station within five minutes.

## Walk 18: CIRCUIT FROM SESTRI LEVANTE — ROMAN ROADS AND OLD SLATE TRAILS

**Distance/time:** 15km/9.3mi; 5h15min

**Grade:** moderate, with an overall ascent/descent of 680m/2230ft; rough terrain and little shade climbing Costa Serba, so start early in hot weather; good tracks, trails, paths and about an hour along lanes without traffic

**Route-finding:** forks are many and waymarks few, so you have to pay attention!

**Equipment:** as pages 12-13

**Refreshments:** Bar/Ristorante Belvedere next to Santa Giulia church (quite expensive, closed Tue); Pizzeria/Osteria del Pino at Cavi Borgo (closed Tue); two bars at Cavi Borgo

**Transport:** 🚌 bus or 🚆 from Chiavari to Sestri Levante via Lavagna (both frequent)

**Map:** as Walk 16, page 79

**Alternative walk: Lavagna to Sestri Levante.** 10km/6.2mi; 3h; easy, with an ascent/descent of 350m/1150ft; about 50min on tarmac roads and sealed tracks. From **Lavagna** RAILWAY STATION follow wide CORSO MAZZINI 300m inland. Turn right behind an old villa onto VIA TEDISIO. Some 50m further on, by a TABERNACLE, take narrow VIA MONTE rising to the left (⎸ SANTA GIULIA, RED DOT WAYMARKS). About five minutes later it levels out, changes to a slate-surfaced trail and joins a small tarmac road. Follow this just 30m straight ahead. At a GATE, turn left on an old cobbled path. It leads uphill between drystone walls enclosing olive groves. Where it meets a track, turn right to pass through the hamlet of **San Benedetto** (**20min**). The trail, now tarmac underfoot, dips through a depression. Some 20m behind the lowest point, turn right on a slate-surfaced path. It rises steadily, initially parallel to the tarmac road for Santa Giulia on the left. Emerging from walled olive groves, you pass some houses on the right, next to the road. Cross the road, heading left. The climbing becomes a little stiffer. With a short swerve to the left you cross a side-road, to arrive at the church of **Santa Giulia** (**1h**). Pick up the main walk at the 3H30MIN-POINT and follow it past the ruins of SANT'ANNA (**2h20min**). At the fork 50m behind the church take the left-hand path (WAY-MARKS: THREE RED DOTS). It descends in hairpin bends, crossing the foundations of two small ROMAN BRIDGES in a valley, where you meet a small road. Follow this parallel to the railway line, crossing under the tracks via the SOTTOPASSAGGIO PIETRA CALANTE. Follow the seaside promenade (LUNGO-MARE) towards Sestri Levante. About 300m further on, cross the VIA AURELIA by heading left and continue along VIALE ROMA to **Sestri Levante** RAILWAY STATION (**3h**).

Between the coastal plains of Sestri Levante and Chiavari the foothills of Monte Capenardo meet the sea, forming a short stretch of steep coast. But this was hardly an insurmountable obstacle for the Roman engineers who built the Via Aurelia from Rome to Provence! At the beginning and the end of this walk you follow a part of this ancient route. In between you climb a barren panoramic slope, cross shady woods and pass through quiet villages and hamlets amid olive groves.

For centuries slate was mined from simple quarries on Monte Capenardo and used, among other things, for roofing and billiard tables. This was men's work. But the women's work was perhaps even harder: the *camelle* or *portatrice del'ardesia* had to bring the slate down to the *leudi* (small coastal sailing boats), balancing up to 50 kilos on their heads. The paths down to the sea were carefully surfaced with slate slabs. This walk follows one of these trails from Santa Giulia to Cavi.

**Start the walk** from the square in front of **Sestri Levante** RAILWAY STATION. Take small VIA OLIVE DI STANGHE diagonally to the right and cross the main road (the modern VIA AURELIA), to get to the seashore. Follow the palm tree-lined seaside promenade (LUNGOMARE) out of town. After about 250m you again cross the VIA AURELIA, before taking an underpass (SOTTOPASSAGGIO PIETRA CALANTE) below the railway line. Continue parallel

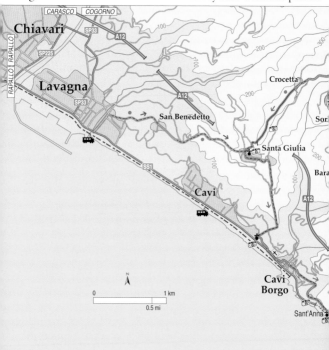

to the tracks on *VIA ROMA ANTICA* to the foothills, where the road bends right. Carry on to the end of the tarmac by a *CAMPSITE*, then follow an earthen trail straight ahead into a small valley with a stream on your right (*THREE RED DOTS*). This is the beginning of the ancient route of the *VIA AURELIA*, laid out in Roman times. The trail rises in three hairpins through low macchia away from the valley, crossing the foundations of two small *ROMAN BRIDGES*. From a ledge near the ruins of *SANT'ANNA* church, which features later in the walk, you enjoy a fine view across the sea to the Sestri Levante Peninsula (**35min**).

Turn right uphill on a stony trail (⌐ *MONTE CAPENARDO 45MIN, RARE RED Ø WAY-MARKS*). It's a steady uphill pull over the eroded rocky slopes of **Costa Serba**, where a fire has destroyed the pine forest. You have little shade but good views. (*Look out for mountain bikers rushing down this breakneck rocky trail.*) After 15 minutes of steep climbing, the path runs through fresh young pines and levels out for 250m. Ignore a path joining from the right and, 100m further on, a path off to the left (**1h10min**). Keep to the well-worn main trail straight ahead, going uphill again, stony underfoot. At a fork, keep slightly right, to enter a Mediterranean macchia forest of holm oaks, strawberry trees and ferns. After about five minutes from the end of the uphill section, you pass a *HOUSE* on the left, where the trail widens out. Some 200m further on you meet a small track, where you turn left. The track runs along the eastern slope of low **Monte Costello** (494m) onto a grassy ridge where it levels off briefly. From this *HIGHEST POINT OF THE WALK* (**1h50min**) you have superb views to the coast and inland to the isolated Apennine mountain ranges.

At the end of the ridge, where the track starts rising again, turn left on a grassy path (*no waymarks*). It descends along the open slope with views to the Portofino Peninsula, then crosses a shady mixed forest. Some 20 minutes down from Monte Costello ridge the trail drops down more steeply for a short way, crossing an open slope of sparse black pines. You go through another forest, on a trail that's easy underfoot.

Bear right in front of an olive grove, to meet a track, where you descend to the right. Within three minutes the track joins the little-used BARASSI–SORLANA ROAD (**2h25min**).

Follow the road towards Sorlana for five minutes. Some 50m past an old FREIGHT ELEVATOR, turn left between crash barriers. Descend a woodland path to an old STONE BRIDGE over a stream. On the far side you rise away from the valley through an olive grove. Some 50m before reaching the first house of a HAMLET, take some steps up to the right, to the end of a side-road. This takes you to the MAIN SORLANA ROAD. Follow this ahead for 100m, to a left-hand bend (**2h40min**), then fork right on a cobbled mule trail next to an old STONE HUT. It rises parallel to the road, changes to a paved footpath, and skirts the upper edge of **Sorlana** village. Pass the white village CHURCH on the left and descend to the far end of the village, where you join the ROAD again (**2h50min**).

Keep to the road for a good 15 minutes, contouring the hillside covered with olive trees. There is little traffic. Some 30m behind a left-hand bend, where a high drystone wall supports the slope, fork right on a path (**3h**). It climbs three minutes through an olive grove, to a small road. Turn left past the few houses of **Crocetta**. On the following left-hand bend, fork right on a tarmac track (RED DOT WAYMARKS). With views to the sea, this runs along the hillside to a GROUP OF HOUSES. Keep to the

left here. Some 200m further on you arrive at HOUSE NUMBER 15, shaded by pines and cypresses. Take the downhill path to the right in front of its gate. Surfaced with slate slabs, this soon joins a road overlooking the densely populated Chiavari plain. Follow this downhill towards **Santa Giulia**'s white clock tower. After three minutes, branch off right on a path leading to the nearby CHURCH (**3h30min**). Have a look inside, to see its rich baroque decoration. *(The Alternative walk joins here.)*

From the church square go down some steps and cross the road below. Continue on a slate walkway going past a line of houses *(no waymarks)*. After traversing a flat terrace with olive trees it rejoins the road. Follow this 100m downhill, to a left-hand bend by some houses, where you continue straight ahead on a descending footpath. It soon passes the old VILLA EREMO SANTA CECILIA

*Slate-surfaced trail between Santa Giulia and Cavi*

(**3h40min**), then squeezes downhill between drystone walls. When you cross a small road, you'll find your ongoing trail 20m to the right, dropping down steps. Soon a smooth, beautifully surfaced slate path takes you between the drystone enclosures of lovely olive plantations. You go past the entrance to a decayed OLD VILLA, then turn right in front of a PINK HOUSE in an olive grove. You cross a ROAD and descend steps to a SECOND ROAD. Follow this to the left, go past **Cavi**'s panoramic CHURCH on the right and down to the main coastal road, once again joining the modern VIA AURELIA (**4h10min**). Continue left on the pedestrian walkway for some 50m, then follow the side-road VIA BRIGATE PARTIGIANI into **Cavi Borgo** — the lower, seaside part of the village. At HOUSE NUMBER 13 take small VIA SAN LEONARDO off to the left, turn right on VIA MILLE IGNOTO, and go past RISTORANTE DEL PINO

to the HOTEL DORIA. Here you cross the side-road for Barassi. About 30m ahead a yellow metal signpost, 'PEDONALE S. ANNA', indicates your ongoing trail.

Take the stepped path rising between some closely-packed houses. Some five minutes up from Cavi Borgo it joins a tarmac track which you follow straight ahead. Soon the track changes to a lovely earthen trail and bears round to the right, uphill. After another short stretch of tarmac you join an old coastal path, which follows the route of the ancient VIA AURELIA. This lovely path contours along the steep slopes between Cavi and Sestri Levante, with fine views down to the sea. After about 10 minutes it arrives at the ruined small church of SANT' ANNA, a panoramic spot for a break (**4h 40min**). Some 50m further on you meet your outgoing route at the 35MIN-POINT. From here retrace your steps back to **Sestri Levante** (**5h15min**).

## Walk 19: FROM BELVEDERE DI PRATOSOPRALACROCE TO GRAMIZZA — DESERTED MOUNTAINS

**Distance/time:** 16km/10mi; 5h15min

**Grade:** moderate-strenuous; overall ascent/descent around 800m/2625ft; the tracks and paths are mostly good underfoot (at the start 40min along a little-trafficked tarmac road),

but because of its length and ascents this is a quite demanding walk

**Route-finding:** fairly easy; waymarking throughout, except for the first 45 minutes

**Equipment:** as pages 12-13; you are in the mountains,

*Approaching Amborzasco*

heavy rain and thunderstorms may occur at any time, so *always be prepared for rainfall*
**Refreshments:** bar at the bus stop in Gramizza (closed Mon); the mountain refuge Rifugio Monte Penna halfway along has a bar and a simple restaurant (open from end Jun to the beginning of Sep and on weekends with good weather for the rest of the year)
**Transport:** 🚐 from Chiavari railway station to Belvedere. *Summer timetable:* Mon-Sat from mid-June to mid-Sep at 10.00, stopping in Borzonasca at 10.39, arriving Belvedere 11.05; back from Gramizza to Chiavari via Borzonasca at 18.21. *Winter timetable:* Mon-Sat from mid-Sep to mid-Jun from Chiavari railway station at 7.30, with change at Borzonasca (8.10/8.15) to Belvedere (8.40); another bus at 10.00 with change at Carasco and Borzonasca (10.40/10.45) to Belvedere (11.10). Back from Gramizza to Chiavari at 16.46 and 18.46 via Borzonasca. For timetables see www.atpesercizio.it
**Map:** Appennino Ligure Sheet 7+8 (1:25,000; Edizioni Multigraphic Firenze)

All the walks in this book have the high Apennines as a constant backdrop. Sometimes we look out to green, wooded slopes, at other times the landscape shows its brown and barren face. In contrast to all the other walks in this book (which keep to the coast), this hike leads deep into the sparsely inhabited and seldom-visited hinterland, rising to a height of 1800 metres. Walking through the unspoilt highlands of the Aveto Nature Reserve 40 kilometres north of Chiavari, you feel yourself far away from the Mediterranean warmth of the Ligurian coast. As you make for Gramizza, you won't pass a village or permanently inhabited house for several hours. There is plenty of variety, too: you'll follow both shady forest trails and narrow paths across open grassy slopes, where on clear days you enjoy superb panoramic views. Because this walk lies between 800 and 1500 metres, it's perfectly feasible in high summer. But it's only possible on workdays, as there are no buses to the starting point on Sundays.

**Start the walk** from the LAST BUS STOP at **Belvedere**, a small hamlet (770m). Follow the provincial road uphill towards PASSO DEL GHIFFI/PASSO DEL BOCCO. There's little traffic. After a good 10 minutes, the road bends sharp left. Keep to the road for another 500 metres, until it is joined by a concrete track coming up from the left. At this point, climb up the bank to an old STONE HUT some 50m away and turn sharp right in front of it. Go uphill across the grassy slope. Behind the PYLON for some low wires, at the edge of a wood, take the path climbing back to the road (**30min**).
Now walk along the road for another 15 minutes. It rises gradually with far-off views to the west. Immediately behind a

right-hand bend through a streambed, in front of a WOODEN SHELTER, turn left on a path (YELLOW SQUARE WAYMARKS). It's a stiff climb over rocky ground up through a small valley. There's a pine forest on your right as you step onto the SADDLE (1150m; **1h**) on the north side of 1237m-high **Monte Ghiffi**.

Here you join the Ligurian long-distance walk ALTA VIA, which you follow north from the saddle (WAYMARKS YELLOW SQUARES AND DOUBLE WHITE STRIPES ON A RED GROUND). The lovely path runs slightly to the right of a long ridge descending from north to south. It climbs gradually, offering far-off panoramic views into the secluded Aveto Mountains with flat-topped Monte Aiona (1703m) and sharply pointed Monte Penna (1735m). Beyond a small forest of mountain pines, the path climbs steeply for five minutes, to a Y-fork on **Passo della Scaletta** (1258m; **1h50min**).

*Leave* the Alta Via here and take the path to the left (☞ PASSO DELLA SPINGARDA, (WAYMARKS YELLOW SQUARES AND RED TRIANGLES). Gently descending through beech woods, it soon enters a deep ravine. Here you cross a foaming stream and carry on uphill, with the watercourse on your right. Three minutes later the path starts rising and winds away from the stream. To the east the steep cliffs of the **Rocca della Scaletta** close off the horizon. When you meet another path (**2h15min**), turn right (WAYMARKS YELLOW SQUARES AND RED CROSSES). After another 10 minutes, beyond a panoramic section

high on the slope, you arrive at an *easily missed* junction: take the path off left (THREE RED DOTS). It climbs steadily over barren slopes to the lower edge of **Prato Mollo**, a wide meadow. After the thaw small streams meander downhill here from the foot of **Monte Aiona**. And when it's foggy — which occurs quite often — it's very like the Scottish Highlands. At the upper edge of the meadow you come to the rather unattractive RIFUGIO MONTE PENNA (1503m; **2h50min**).

Follow the wide track that starts at the left of the building. Some 100m along, take a smaller track off right, going through a barrier (HOLLOW YELLOW DIAMOND WAYMARKS AS FAR AS GRAMIZZA). It rises gently and within 10 minutes takes you to the **Passo della Spingarda** (1551m), the HIGHEST POINT OF THE WALK. From now on it's almost all downhill. Keep to the main trail, which soon passes a SPRING on the left. Beyond a pine and beech forest, you come to a T-junction some 25 minutes down from the pass. Go 50m to the right, turn left behind a WOODEN HUT, and cross a stream. You emerge on a small meadow signposted **Moglia Negretta**. It's a nice place for a break, with another SPRING (1382m, **3h30min**).

Follow the signpost 'GRAMIZZA' to the start of a woodland trail. It descends gradually north, with good views towards the pyramid of **Monte Penna**. Ten minutes down from Moglia Negretta, on a left-hand bend, take a path straight ahead into the forest. Turning left, it becomes very stony underfoot, before rejoining the main trail, which now loses height. Watch for a SPRING WITH AN IRON TUBE on the right: some 30m further down, take a path off right, to cross a stream after 30m (**4h10min**).

Follow the adjacent path downstream, soon going through a GATE (by a small Madonna in a rock face). Accompanied by the sound of the rushing stream you traverse a damp and dark conifer wood. Emerging, you pass a drystone wall on your left and reach the upper end of the **Amborzasco** meadows. Past a stone HUT WITH A SMALL TABERNACLE bear left, to cross the grassy slope (pathless) to another STONE HUT 200m away. Behind this hut, turn right on a small track, descending through fields and meadows towards Amborzasco with its slender church tower. The trail passes a CHAPEL and enters the village. Keep straight on to the main church (877m; (**5h**).

Follow the main village road some 200m downhill. On a sharp right-hand bend, take a footpath straight ahead, crossing the road 70m further on. Descend a grassy trail, which bends left and again joins the Amborzasco road. Around 30m downhill take a forest trail off left. Within five minutes it takes you down to the main road through the hamlet of **Gramizza**. From here it's only a few metres straight ahead, to the BUS STOP on the right-hand side of the road, opposite a bar (765m; **5h15min**).

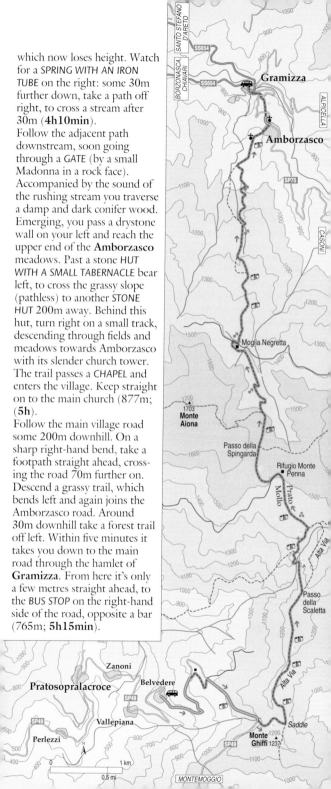

## Walk 20: FROM MADONNA DI MONTALLEGRO TO ZOAGLI — HIGH ABOVE THE TIGULLIO GULF

**Distance/time:** 9km/5.6mi; 3h05min

**Grade:** easy-moderate; some short descents over stony ground need attention; overall ascent about 100m/330ft and descent 700m/2300ft

**Route-finding:** easy on the waymarked route as far as the Anchetta Pass; for the rest of the walk some care is needed, as there are no waymarks

**Equipment:** as pages 12-13

**Refreshments:** bar/restaurant five minutes from Montallegro; alimentari/bar 50m below San Pietro church

**Transport:** 🚠 funicular from Rapallo to Montallegro: every half hour from 9.00-12.30 and 14.00-17.30; it starts from Piazza Solari a good five minutes walk to the northeast of Rapallo railway station (follow the 'Funivia' signs). 🚌 or bus (several daily from Rapallo railway station to Montallegro). Return on 🚌 train or 🚌 bus (every hour from Zoagli to Rapallo or Chiavari); buses stop above Zoagli's centre, on Via Aurelia

**Map:** Carta dei Sentieri e Rifugi, Appennino Ligure Sheets 6+8 (1:25,000, Edizioni Multigraphic Firenze)

**Shorter walk: Semorile– Passo Monte Anchetta– Zoagli.** 6km/3.7mi; 2h10min; easy, with an ascent of 250m/820ft and descent of 520m/1700ft. Take a 🚌 bus from Zoagli town centre (from Via Luigi Morello near the round main piazza): departures for Semorile on workdays at 7.20, 9.45, 12.00, 13.50, on Sundays at 7.30, 10.00. From Zoagli an old trading route leads across the Anchetta Pass into the Fontanabuona Valley. The section from Semorile to the ridge is probably the best preserved mule trail in all of Liguria. It winds steadily and evenly uphill. From the LAST

*Along the ridge before Monte Anchetta*

BUS STOP in the small village of **Semorile** (270m) follow the road you came in on 100m back downhill. Then turn sharp left on a concrete footpath (" MONTE ANCHETTA). It rises to the upper houses of the small village. Keep right here and go past B&B LE TERRAZZE SUL MARE on the left. Leaving the village, the path swings left, then right. It crosses olive groves (well kept near the village, abandoned further up). About 15 minutes from Semorile you enter a thick forest of pines and sweet chestnut. Winding uphill, you constantly gain height. Beyond a 'Mediterranean jungle' you step onto **Passo Anchetta** (474m; **35min**), where you meet a small tarmac road. Turn right on the road and follow the main walk from the 1H25MIN-POINT to **Zoagli** (**2h10min**).

T he Sanctuary of Madonna di Montallegro (612m), served by the Rapallo funicular, is a good starting point for a pleasant walk with no appreciable ascents. From the church the route first follows a wooded ridge, which offers superb views across the Tigullio Gulf. A long descent on old cobbled trails, flights of steps and typical Ligurian walkways takes you down to the sea. The walk ends at unimpressive (but nevertheless pleasant) Zoagli. This small coastal town is rich in subtropical vegetation and has a little pebble beach, where you could take a swim. Over the centuries Zoagli has been a centre for luxurious silks and damasks. Two manufacturers (Seteria Cordani and Seteria Gaggioli) still carry out this traditional weaving.

**Start the walk** from the upper FUNICULAR STATION. Go up the steps to the nearby sanctuary of MADONNA DI MONTALLEGRO (612m). Walk to the left of the church and turn right behind it (RED SQUARE WAYMARKS). A paved footpath lined by the STATIONS OF THE CROSS leads within three minutes to the ALBERGO/RISTORANTE PELLE-GRINO, with a pleasant panoramic terrace bar. Cross the terrace and carry on straight ahead along a more or less flat old cobbled pilgrim's trail below shady holm oaks. About 20 minutes from the *albergo* the view opens up north to the high Apennines. *Take care here,* as you have to turn off left on a smaller path (30min; still RED SQUARE WAYMARKS).

The path rises steeply over some rocks for 30 metres and then contours along the inland slopes of **Monte Castello** (665m). Arriving at the south-eastern side of the mountain, the sea comes into view. From a flat rock here you have to descend steeply over scree for 20 metres. Then you descend gently along the south side of the ridge, enjoying splendid sea views. After walking alongside a drystone wall you re-enter the forest. The path, in places stony underfoot, leads to a Y-fork by the stone pillar tabernacle ORATORIO LA COLLA (525m; **1h**). Turn right, uphill. This small path winds its way along the wooded ridge. About 10 minutes from the tabernacle it

starts to drop steeply and is stony underfoot for five minutes. The descent ends on the **Passo Anchetta**, by a small tarmac road (474m; **1h 25min**). *(The shorter walk from Semorile joins here.)*

Keep straight ahead on the ascending road. Five minutes later take a side-road to the right, *leaving the square red waymarks.* The tarmac ends very soon on a grassy ridge, with far-reaching views down to the coast. Keep to the left of a BAR/TRATTORIA (only open on weekends), then take a path starting at the right of a track and a METAL HUT (▪ LA MADO-NETTA 15 MIN, SAN PIETRO 50 MIN, NO WAYMARKS). This lovely trail descends along the seaside slopes, passing old terraces with drystone walls. Entering the woods it changes to a cobbled mule trail and descends gradually to the small church of LA MADONETTA, hidden in the forest (**1h50min**).

Ignore the path downhill right signposted for Zoagli. Keep left and carry on along the old cobbled trail, through an oak forest. Leaving the woods you enjoy a superb view across the Tigullio Gulf. Pass a RED HOUSE on the left, and turn right 30m further on. Follow VIA LONGAROLA downhill past YELLOW HOUSE on your right (**2h05min**). Keep to the stepped footpath, dropping seaward through olive groves. At a road crossing, go 10m to the right and take another flight of steps downhill (▪ CHIESA DI SAN PIETRO). Within three minutes you arrive at a group of houses by **San Pietro** CHURCH (**2h25min**)

Behind the church, next to HOUSE NUMBER 80, turn right, to descend the stepped concret footpath SCALINATA MONTÀ (DIAGONALLY DIVIDED RED AND WHITE SQUARE WAYMARKS, ROUTE 5-C). Keep left at a fork, to join the small road coming from San Pietro. Follow this down past a huge castle-like villa, built in 1914 by the Italian writer Sem Benelli. Today it houses the showrooms of the traditional silk manu-facturer Cordani. About 100m further on, by two small car parks behind HOUSE NUMBER 15, turn left on a path. It soon meets the main coastal road, the Via Aurelia, at the upper end of Zoagli.

*Cross carefully* and, 50m down-hill, take the small station road off left (■ STAZIONE). Twenty metres further on, turn right on the stepped footpath VIA G MAMELI. It swings left below old villas, through abundant subtropical vegetation — palm trees, bougainvillaea, khaki and bananas — and joins the pedestrian lane VIA GARIBALDI. About 30m further on, turn sharp left and follow a stepped lane down to **Zoagli** STATION (**2h50min**). Take the flight of steps opposite, go through the tunnel under the rail lines, and join LUNGOMARE CANEVARO. This lovely concrete walkway follows the shoreline below steep cliffs. It leads to the PEBBLE BEACH under the big RAILWAY BRIDGE by Zoagli's MAIN SQUARE (**3h**).

Take Via Garibaldi from the square back to the STATION or go past the main CHURCH and CEMETERY on the right, uphill to the VIA AURELIA, where buses for Rapallo or Chiavari stop.

*Holm oak forest on the ridge*

## Walk 21: FROM RUTA TO MONTE MANICO DEL LUM[E] AND SANT'ANDREA DI FOGGIA — BLUE HORIZONS

**Distance/time:** 15km/9.3mi; 5h30min

**Grade:** strenuous; overall ascent 680m/2230ft, descent 850m/2790ft; you must be sure-footed (some narrow and exposed paths, especially on the detour from the 3h05min-point to the top of Monte Manico del Lume). Avoid rainy weather, when the stony ground becomes slippery, as well as hot days, since there is little shade en route.

**Route-finding:** relatively easy; waymarks throughout

**Equipment:** as pages 12-13

**Refreshments:** none en route

**Transport:** 🚌 bus from Rapallo, Santa Margherita Ligure or Camogli to Ruta (every 50 minutes on workdays, fewer buses on Sundays). Return on 🚌 bus from Sant'Andrea di Foggia to Rapallo railway station (on workdays at 12.46, 14.25, 19.00, 19.42). (There are more buses from San Pietro, half an hour's walk from Sant'Andrea: go down the road some 150m, to a right-hand bend, take a short-cut path to the left, and continue along the road to the church of San Pietro (with a bar next door); buses leave from here for Santa Margherita Ligure via Rapallo every 50min, on Sundays only at 15.00, 17.00, 19.00)

**Map:** as Walk 20, page 96

**Shorter walks**

1 Ruta–Passo del Gallo–Monte Orsena–Ruta. 10km/ 6.2mi; 3h40min; moderate, with an ascent/descent of 420m/1375ft. Follow the main walk to the **Passo del Gallo** (492m; **1h45min**). Then retrace your steps 100m, back to a fork. Keep straight on here, *leaving the two red circles*, to follow a smaller path slightly to the left. This rises on the northern ridge of Monte Orsena (*FAINT HOLLOW RED SQUARES*). After a steep ascent through a small wood, the path briefly levels out, then climbs again. Having crossed small overgrown meadows and patches of woodland, you finally arrive at the secluded *SANTUARIO DI CARAVAGGIO* at the top of **Monte Orsena** (615m; **2h15min**). The church, completely rebuilt in the 20th century, is of little interest, but the panoramic views from here are superb. Descend from the sanctuary by a flight of steps to a tarred square with a *PAINTED YELLOW H*. Turn sharp right on a stone-laid pilgrim's trail (*no waymarks*). It leads gradually downhill to the grassy rest area at the *1H15MIN-POINT* in the main walk (**2h35min**). Retrace your outward route back to **Ruta** (**3h40min**).

2 Omit the detour from **Passo della Serra** to **Monte Manico del Lume**. 4h30min; moderate-strenuous, about 220m less climbing than the main walk.

This splendid long walk between the coast and the mountains follows high panoramic ridges for hours, with plenty of splendid views down to the sea. The highlight is Monte Manico del Lume, one of the best vantage points on the entire Riviera. But climbing its steep summit demands some rock clambering experience — so if you don't have a head for heights and are not absolutely sure-footed, omit the last part of the walk (Shorter walk 2). Even without scaling the Monte Manico del Lume summit, this walk takes you far from modern civilisation and is definitely rewarding.

**Start the walk** in **Ruta** from the central BUS STOP some 50m west of the ROAD TUNNEL below the pass between Rapallo and Recco. Take the side-road rising to the left (seen in direction of the tunnel entrance when coming from Camogli), signposted for SAN MARTINO. After about five minutes the road passes the small medieval CHIESA VECCHIA on the left. Immediately past this church, turn left on the concrete VIA CARAVAGGIO (TWO HOLLOW RED CIRCLES). This walkway rises past some houses and changes to an earthen path. It's a steady uphill pull along a ridge covered with holm oaks. Every now and then far-off views down to the sea open out. Cross a TRACK (**50min**) and go straight ahead, keeping to the ridge. The path now runs level or rises very gently. Narrowing, it contours the steep western slopes of **Monte Ampola**. You then come to a grassy rest area (496m; **1h 15min**) at the foot of **Monte Orsena**, where the SANTUARIO DI CARAVAGGIO stands at the top.

Ignore a trail uphill to the right for the sanctuary and keep straight ahead on the way-marked path (▪ PASSO DELLA SPINAROLA). It runs along the western flanks of Monte Orsena. For a while it descends a little through deciduous forest, then starts climbing onto the open ridge. A grassy trail takes you up to the sign-posted **Passo del Gallo** (492m; **1h45min**), a lovely panoramic picnic spot.

Continue straight ahead to the north along the ridge. A good 10 minutes up from Passo del Gallo, turn right at a fork (530m), *leaving* the main trail with the two red circles. Bear right again at another fork 50m further on (HOLLOW RED TRIANGLES). The narrow path rises gently along the southern slopes of **Monte Bello** for a good five minutes. Then it turns left and climbs steeply about 100 metres over rocky terrain. From the end of this stiff climb keep right. After a short descent and re-ascent, the path levels out and contours along the barren southeast side of Monte Bello (713m) and **Monte Borgo** (732m). You enjoy splendid views down to Rapallo Bay, but the path, narrow in places, demands attention too. In early summer broom colours the slopes a glowing yellow.

Making your way through dense ferns, you finally reach a

*Sant'Andrea di Foggia*

SADDLE to the east of Monte Borgo. Keep straight on for five minutes, following a faint path about 10m to the right of the ridge. At the far end of the saddle, the **Passo della Serra (643m; 2h50min)**, you meet a well-worn path edged with flat stone slabs, coming up from the right, from Chignero. This is your ongoing route, but first you could take a strenuous but very rewarding detour to a nearby summit: cross the old trail and follow a small path uphill along the open ridge (still RED TRIANGLES). At a fork

fives minutes up from Passo della Serra, take the path to the right. Walk under some wires and head uphill on stone slabs to a FIRST VIEWPOINT at the upper end of the ridge (**3h05min**). A fixed CHAIN helps you clamber down onto the saddle below. Then, with the aid of FIXED ROPES, you can haul yourself steeply up to the top of **Monte Manico del Lume (801m; 3h20min)**. From this summit, covered in layers of white rock, the views over the coast and up to the inland mountains are thrilling.

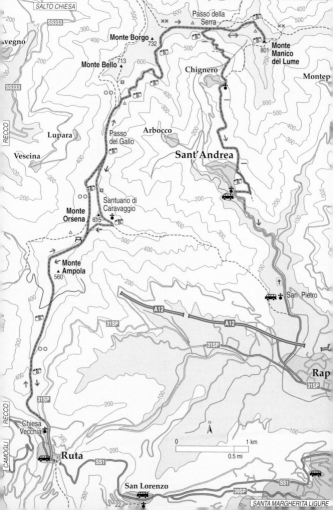

*Below Monte Orsena*

Retrace your steps to **Passo della Serra** (**3h50min**). Turn left on the old trail downhill to Chignero (*RED STRIPES*). At first it descends gradually. When it veers left, there are fine views over Chignero's small church to the Portofino Peninsula. Some 10 min down from the pass, the trail becomes stony and steeper. After entering an oak wood, it swings left and levels out for about 150m on a tree-covered terrace, before continuing steeply downhill on a flight of old stone steps. The steps end at a T-junction by a big *DRYSTONE WALL* on the right (**4h15min**). Turn left on a level path. It soon crosses a rocky streambed on a small *WOODEN FOOTBRIDGE*, turns right and descends through a thick forest at the left of the valley. Leaving the woods, you arrive at the small *CHURCH* of **Chignero** (385m; **4h30min**).

The continuing route starts at the right of the church: descend steps (still *RED STRIPE WAYMARKS*). The path swings right to the lower part of the village, where it meets a concrete walkway. Turn left here, and left again at the next two forks just 5m apart. You pass an old *STONE HOUSE* on the right with a *RED WAYMARK* on its corner. After the last houses the walkway changes to a fairly wide but little-used cobbled mule trail, once the main route through the valley. It descends gradually along the eastern slopes to the upper edge of an olive grove. It becomes steep and stony for a short way, before joining a *ROAD AT THE UPPER EDGE OF SANT'ANDREA* (**5h05min**). Turn left and follow the narrowing road uphill. Down in the bottom of the valley, Sant'Andrea's red church tower appears, your final destination. The tarmac road levels out and reduces to a small concrete track. Keep straight on to a *LAST HOUSE*. Turn right and drop down a stepped footpath lined with cypresses. You meet the valley road and the *BUS STOP* by the *CHURCH* of **Sant'Andrea di Foggia** (95m; **5h30min**).

# The Portofino Peninsula

## a gem of nature

*Camogli: Santa Maria Assunta and Castello Dragone*

**A**s in the more famous Cinque Terre further south, the small mountain range on the peninsula between Camogli and Portofino has been protected from overdevelopment: the area has been a nature reserve since 1935. So there is no road along the coastal mountains, which plunge with steep reddish cliffs into the sea. The small peninsula, rising to a maximum height of 612 metres, is criss-crossed by many way-marked walking trails, some of them ancient cobbled mule trails. They make this small piece of natural coast-line an idyllic hiking destination.

There is a map of the peninsula on pages 108-109. The northern gateway to the promontory is the highly picturesque small harbour town of **Camogli**. Its coastal promenade is lined by tall 200-year-old buildings reflecting the sun in warm yellows, oranges and reds. In a sense they're pre-industrial skyscrapers: Camogli's ship owners were among the most powerful European merchants in the 19th century. They owned almost 1000 ships — twice as many as Genoa. One source of their wealth was their founding, in 1853, of the world's first maritime insurance against loss of freight and ships. The houses, up to seven stories high, are a reminder of this glorious past. The older medieval town centre is located around the photogenic main church, SANTA MARIA ASSUNTA, and the 12th-century CASTELLO DRAGONE. They stand on a rocky ledge above the small harbour bay, where traditional wooden fishing boats still anchor.

**San Fruttuoso** is a secluded small bay on the southern coast of the peninsula. In the eighth century a few monks from Spain, fleeing the Arabs, arrived here with the relics of the martyr Saint Fructuosus. They built a monastery which became very powerful from the 11th to the 13th century. San Fruttuoso, which even today has no roads, is without doubt a fascinating place with a magic touch — but all that is lost on hot summer days, when it's invaded by day-trippers who come in by boat to bathe at the little beach in front of the abbey.

Coming from the sea, what you first notice is the 700-year-old ABBOT'S PALACE. The CHURCH behind it is one of the oldest in Liguria but has been renovated many times. The massive TORRE DORIA towers above the bay; it was built in 13th century by the powerful Doria clan of Genoa.

**Portofino** is very famous, beautiful, expensive … and artificial. It was 'discovered' in 1870 by the British consul in Genoa, Montague Yeats-Brown, who was highly enthusiastic about the charm of the village and its natural surroundings. He bought and renovated the castle. Following his example, many other European aristocrats settled in idyllic Portofino. It became one of the most exclusive little Riviera harbours and was visited by many famous people — from the German philosopher Friedrich Nietzsche and the French writer Guy de Maupassant to American movie stars like Frank Sinatra, Elizabeth Taylor and Humphrey Bogart.

The main reason for coming here is to admire a traditional Ligurian harbour town untouched by modern development. Take a walk to the church of SAN GIORGIO or the CASTELLO BROWN overlooking the picturesque little bay lined by multicoloured old façades. But take care when visiting Portofino's bars and restaurants — they are all very overpriced.

## Getting about

Only **local or regional trains** stop at Camogli. On workdays there are trains every 30-60 minutes for Recco/Genoa and for Santa Margherita Ligure, Rapallo, Chiavari and Sestri Levante (some of which go on to the Cinque Terre and La Spezia).

On workdays there are **buses** at least every 50 minutes (on Sundays about hourly) from Rapallo to Genoa's railway station via Recco and from Santa Margherita Ligure to Camogli; the two lines are timed to arrive at Ruta simultaneously, to allow for a quick change. Half-hourly buses run from Santa Margherita Ligure railway station to Portofino. For timetables see www.atpesercizio.it.

**Parking** at Portofino is impossible during high season. The road from Santa Margherita Ligure is also normally blocked by traffic jams. So it is the best to take a boat. Camogli centre is also short on parking places; in summer you have to leave your car at nearby Recco and take a bus or train into town.

The best way to explore the peninsula is by **boat**. Boats run all year round 3-12 times a day from Camogli harbour to San Fruttuoso; for timetables see www. golfoparadiso.it. From May to October the boats also ply from Rapallo via Santa Margherita Ligure to Portofino and San Fruttuoso; for timetables see www. traghettiportofino.it.

## Walk planning

Walks 22-25 will give you a complete picture of the Portofino Peninsula, but Walk 25 is quite demanding.

**Out of area walks:** Camogli is a perfect starting point for the routes across the peninsula, and also for Walks 21 from Ruta and 26 and 27 from Genoa (only 35 minutes away by train). And any walk starting no further south than Monterosso can be done as a day-trip.

## Accommodation

Forget Portofino with its astronomic prices. **Camogli** is a much better base. Central HOTEL CASMONA★★★ has good rooms, some with balconies (www.casmona.com, 125-185 €). Nearby, friendly LA CAMOGLIESE★★ is good value; doubles from 70-115 € (www.lacamogliese.it).

## Walk 22: FROM SAN LORENZO DELLA COSTA TO PORTOFINO — ACROSS THE PENINSULA

**Distance/time:** 10km/6.2mi; 3h
**Grade:** easy, with an ascent of 370m/1200ft and descent of 560m/1835ft
**Route-finding:** fairly easy; there are many forks, but the route is waymarked throughout except from Portofino to Punta del Capo; there are also green/white signposts at crossings and forks. Waymarks: hollow red diamonds to Gaixella, red squares to Pietre Strette, from there red triangles and red Ts, and for the final descent to Portofino back to red squares.
**Equipment:** as pages 12-13
**Refreshments:** none en route; bar at San Lorenzo della Costa next to the church; pricey bars and restaurants at Portofino
**Transport:** 🚌 to San Lorenzo della Costa: buses from Rapallo to Recco and from Santa Margherita Ligure to Camogli stop at San Lorenzo, at the eastern edge of the village, behind Trattoria degli Amici and *before* the main church, so press the bell in time! Return on 🚌 bus from Portofino to Santa Margherita Ligure (half-hourly) or, from May-Oct 🚤 there are boats from Portofino to Santa Margherita Ligure and Rapallo
**Map:** Carta dei Sentieri, Monte di Portofino, Sheet GE-38 (1:25,000, Edizioni del Magistero). A leaflet, 'Vie e Sentieri del Monte di Portofino', usually available at tourist offices in Rapallo, Santa Margherita Ligure and Camogli, gives a good overview of trails on the Portofino Peninsula.
**Alternative walks**
**1** from **Gaixella** to **Pietre Strette** you could take a 1h15min longer, but more beautiful route via **Toca**; see Walk 24 on page 115 from the 1h25min-point; this involves around 150m/490ft additional ascent/descent.
**2** from **Pietre Strette** you could follow Walk 24 (page 116) down to **San Fruttuoso**.

This easy and varied walk takes you across the beautiful Portofino Peninsula. It follows old mule trails and paved footpaths through farmland with lush gardens and Mediterranean forests. There are many places with far-reaching views down to the sea. The walk ends at the highly fashionable small harbour town of Portofino, one of the most picturesque — but also most expensive — places in all of Italy.

**Start the walk** from the BUS STOP in **San Lorenzo della Costa:** follow the main road towards Recco for about 100m, then go up the steps into PIAZZA LUIGI MAZZINI with the parish church, the CHIESA DI SAN LORENZO (195 m). Be sure to look inside this richly decorated baroque church. On the left wall you can admire a masterpiece of Renaissance painting, a triptychon created in 1499 by the Flemish artist Hans Memling.
From the square go uphill on the small paved road to the nearby ORATORIO DELL'SUF-FRAGIO E MORTE and take the lane to the right of this chapel (HOLLOW RED DIAMOND WAY-MARKS). It soon narrows to a

stepped footpath, which passes a TALL OLD VILLA on the right. A good five minutes up from San Lorenzo you join a small country road, rising smoothly with views down to the Tigullio Gulf. After 10 minutes the road turns right and gets steeper. Some 50m further on, on a left-hand bend, take the stepped footpath climbing straight ahead. At the end of the steps, where the RUINS OF AN OLD FARMHOUSE and the big TRANSMITTER at Portofino Vetta come into sight on the left, turn left on an old cobbled path. It passes the scattered houses and gardens of the panoramic hamlet **Dolcina Alta** on the eastern slopes. Within five minutes the old path meets a TRACK coming up from the left (**30min**). Turn right here (▪ PORTOFINO VETTA, HOLLOW RED DIAMOND WAYMARKS). After 50m the track leads into a small stretch of woodland, where you fork left on an old stepped path. It rises along the well-maintained gardens of a nicely situated

*Near Ghidelli*

isolated VILLA on your left. Some 50m above the villa the path heads left across a flat grassy terrace, then bears right and climbs through the woods with some short zigzags. At the foot of the TRANSMITTER at **Portofino Vetta** the path joins a flat track. Follow this to the left (▪ PIETRE STRETTE, RED SQUARE WAYMARKS). About 100m further on you arrive at place signposted '**Gaixella**' (405m; **45min**). WALK 24, rising from Camogli, joins from the right here. Keep ahead on the main trail marked by HOLLOW RED CIRCLES. Some 100m from Gaixella, you come to a fork with signposts. Keep left. *(But for the longer Alternative walk via Toca branch off right here, following signs for 'Paradiso/Semaforo Nuova'.)* It's an easy walk in the shade of trees to the conglomerate rock

## Golfo Paradiso

San Rocco
Mortola
San Nicolo
Punta Chiappa
Porto Pidocchio
Punta Chiappa
Toca
Semaforo Nuovo
Bunker
Punta del Buco
Cala dell'O

0        1 km
0.5 mi

boulders of **Pietre Strette**. Behind them you come to a REST AREA with wooden benches and tables and a tap with drinking water (452m; **1h**). Several waymarked walking routes come together here at Pietre Strette. Going 30m downhill to the right you would join Walk 24 coming from Toca and descending to San Fruttuoso Bay. But heading towards Portofino, keep straight ahead on the main trail (☛ PORTOFINO MARE, RED TRIANGLE WAYMARKS). Around 150 m beyond Pietre Strette fork right on a smaller path (☛ FELCIARA, BASE O, RED TRIANGLE WAYMARKS). It's a pleasant walk above the sea along the edge of a macchia forest full of holm oaks. At the Y-fork at **Felciara** (436m; **1h15min**), ignore the left turn signposted for 'Bocche' by keeping slightly to the right (☛ PORTOFINO MARE VIA PRATO/GHIDELLI, STILL RED TRIANGLES).

From Felciara the path zigzags downhill to another fork at **Ghidelli** within 10 minutes, where you abandon the red triangles by turning left (☛ PORTOFINO MARE, RED 'T' WAYMARKS). You now walk on a narrow, but always clearly visible path, undulating along the seaside slope with fine views. The path ends by joining the MAIN TRAIL DESCENDING FROM PIETRE STRETTE (**1h40min**). Now follow this main route to the right, walking downhill on a well-engineered trail of natural stones (☛ OLMI, RED SQUARE WAYMARKS AS FAR AS PORTOFINO). A good five minutes later you pass the first houses of the spread-out

*Portofino: the setting could not be lovelier*

hamlet of **Olmi**. The trail, now covered with stone slabs, steadily loses height through open countryside with olive groves and scattered farmhouses. Ignore two left turns for Mulino del Gassetta. *(The second one, with red cross waymarks, is Walk 23 coming up from Santa Margherita Ligure.)* Turn left in front of an exposed REST AREA on the ridge, with a wooden table and benches (220m; **1h55min**), descending steeply for a short time. Under 10 minutes later you pass SAN SEBASTIANO.

Continue from this chapel on a small road, enjoying fine views towards blue Tigullio Gulf. Lush vegetation — pines, cypresses, olives, fig, palm, and lemon trees — edges the route. When the road bends left (**2h 15min**) go straight ahead on a stepped footpath. It hairpins down to the UPPER EDGE OF **Portofino**. Cross the MAIN ROAD and follow a lane down past a CHURCH on the left, to the harbour (**2h25min**).

Take a short detour to the Punta del Capo for more fine views: cross the harbour PIAZZA diagonally to the right and ascend narrow SALITA SAN GIORGIO lane to the CHIESA DI SAN GIORGIO, a fine viewpoint. A paved footpath leads from here further uphill to the entrance to the CASTELLO DI SAN GIORGIO (or CASTELLO BROWN), visible from below. The airy terrace of this Genoese castle offers even better views over **Portofino Bay**. From the entrance gate follow an ongoing footpath to the east. It ends within 10 minutes by the white LIGHTHOUSE on the promontory of **Punta del Capo**. (A small bar opens here during the tourist season.) From here you enjoy an extensive view of the **Tigullio Gulf**.

Retrace your steps to the Portofino harbour PIAZZA. Walking to the left of the HOTEL EDEN, you will come to the BUS STOP FOR SANTA MARGHERITA LIGURE (**3h**).

## Walk 23: FROM SANTA MARGHERITA LIGURE TO SAN FRUTTUOSO — A MONASTERY IN A SECLUDED BAY

**See also photos pages 65, 116**
**Distance/time:** 9km/5.6mi; 2h45min
**Grade:** easy-moderate, with an ascent/descent of 350m/ 1150ft; the steep section from Base 0 down to San Fruttuoso is not very difficult, but needs attention, especially when wet
**Route-finding:** fairly easy; waymarks throughout; green/ white signposts at crossings and forks. Waymarks: red crosses for the first half of the walk, double red dots for the second half
**Equipment:** as pages 12-13
**Refreshments:** simple bar/ restaurant at the Mulino del Gassetta (open Jun to Sep); bars and restaurants at San Fruttuoso (pricey, except for Ristorante Da Giovanni)
**Transport, Map:** see Walk 22, page 107
**Map:** as Walk 22, page 107

This rewarding walk starts in the elegant coastal town of Santa Margherita Ligure and ends in an isolated bay, only accessible on foot or by boat. Here, below steep wooded slopes, a few simple houses gather around a Genoese watchtower and a monastery founded in the early Middle Ages. San Fruttuoso is without doubt one of the most fascinating places on the Italian Riviera. The first half of the route follows old trails through lovely farmland of small country houses and colourful gardens. The second half runs along a panoramic coastal trail high above the sea. With a steep final descent you arrive at the bay of San Fruttuoso, a good place for a swim in clear blue water.

**Start the walk** by leaving **Santa Margherita** STATION: walk right for 50m, go down steps, cross the main road, and proceed along the palm-shaded seaside promenade. At the far southern end of Santa Margherita harbour, where you'll see smart yachts anchored, cross the PORTOFINO COASTAL ROAD and take the small street SALITA MONTEBELLO (⊩ NOZA-REGO, OLMI, RED CROSS WAY-MARKS). This leads uphill towards the tower of a large MANOR HOUSE 100m away. At its entrance gate the street bends right and reduces to a stepped lane too small for automobiles. It rises between the garden walls and scattered villas, narrowing to a concrete footpath lined by some olive trees. Then it joins the tarmac VIA MARINAI D'ITALIA by a chapel, the CAPELLETTA DELLA NEVE (**25min**).

Go up the small road for about 100m and then fork left on a path with railings running parallel to the road (⊩ MULINO DEL GASSETTA/GAVE/OLMI, STILL RED CROSS WAYMARKS). At HOUSE NUMBER 12 it turns left, goes up some steps and carries on as an old cobbled mule trail with a drystone wall on the right. Within 10 minutes the trail rises to a broader trail, which you follow to the left (⊩ GAVE). The wide trail narrows to a cobbled path offering far-off views across the Tigullio Gulf. You then come to a fork

30m before the small CHURCH of **Gave** (170m; **45min**). Turn right (☛ OLMI). About 20m further on, ignore the right turn for 'Il Frate'. An old cart track, built from natural stones, leads you through the scattered houses and lush green gardens of Gave. After a left-hand bend across the (normally dry) **Acqua Morta** stream (**1h**) the path rises steeply for 10 minutes through a small forest of oaks. From the end of the ascent it follows the upper edge of an olive plantation to a shady REST AREA with wooden tables and benches. Nearby is the MULINO DEL GASSETTA, a rebuilt old water mill (**1h15min**). In front of the building is a SPRING with drinking water, inside a simple bar/restaurant (seasonal opening).

At the fork 100m down from the Mulino del Gassetta, keep right on a paved footpath (☛ OLMI). Within five minutes, at a T-junction, turn left on a wider path (☛ SAN SEBASTIANO/ PORTOFINO MARE, RED SQUARE WAYMARKS). This is the main walking trail across the peninsula from Ruta to Portofino Bay. In three minutes it takes you downhill to a crossroads by an exposed REST AREA on the ridge (220m; **1h25min**). The trail to Portofino, marked by red squares, turns off left before the wooden picnic benches (see Walk 22 on page 109), but the more exciting route to San Fruttuoso forks off right *behind* the benches (☛ SAN FRUTTUOSO, DOUBLE RED DOT WAYMARKS).

The paved trail dips through a hollow, passes a small pond on the left, then circles to the left and ascends to the nearby farmhouse of PRATO (240m). Take the steps to the right in front of the building. Two minutes later you join the old coastal route to San Fruttuoso. The trail, mostly flat, runs high above the sea. This delightful path, easy underfoot, winds its way through evergreen Mediterranean woods with pines, holm oaks, bush heather, broom and strawberry trees. At several places you enjoy far-reaching views over the steep coast with its reddish-brown rock formations. After around 15 minutes from Prato, you cross a small stream. Some 20 minutes later you arrive at a place signposted 'BASE 0' (225m; **2h05min**), a World War II defense post.

The steep descent to San Fruttuoso starts here. Zigzagging down, mostly in shade, you steadily lose height. About 10 minutes down from Base 0 you

*Between Olmi and San Fruttuoso*

catch a first glimpse of the blue bay, the abbey and the watchtower far below. It takes another 20 minutes to reach the seashore and the first houses of **San Fruttuoso** hamlet. Go through an ARCH, to join a concrete walkway. It circles the bay, to the CHURCH AT SAN FRUTTUOSO MONASTERY (**2h45min**). Walk through the bar Da Giovanni, to the BEACH shown on page 116 and JETTIES on the western side of the bay.

# Walk 24: FROM CAMOGLI TO SAN FRUTTUOSO — MULE TRAILS ACROSS THE PORTOFINO PENINSULA

**Distance/time:** 12km/7.4mi; 3h50min

**Grade:** moderate, with an overall ascent/descent of around 600m/1970ft; easy climbing and good underfoot up to Pietre Strette, but from there old mule trail to San Fruttuoso Bay, which descends 450m/1475ft, is hard on the knees

**Route-finding:** easy; way-marks throughout; green/white signposts at crossings and forks. Waymarks: hollow red circles and two red dots to San Rocco, just hollow red circles to Gaixella, from there red stripe with dot plus two hollow red triangles to Toca, just red triangles to Pietre Strette, finally hollow red circles to San Fruttuoso

**Equipment:** as pages 12-13;

walking sticks are helpful for the descent from Pietre Strette

**Refreshments:** bar in the grocer's shop *(alimentari)* at San Rocco; bar and restaurants at San Fruttuoso (pricey except for Ristorante Da Giovanni)

**Transport:** 🚢 ferry from San Fruttuoso back to Camogli (3-12 a day all year round; for timetables see www.golfopara diso.it, from Oct to Mar last departure at 16.00!)

**Map:** as Walk 22, page 107

**Shorter walk: omit the detour around Monte Portofino.** 7.5km/4.7mi; 2h40min; easy-moderate, with 150m/425ft less ascent/descent than the main walk. After Gaixella, keep to the main trail marked by red squares. In less than 20 minutes you reach Pietre Strette.

For the most part this walk follows an old trail which was once an important route; it leads from the harbour town of Camogli to the isolated bay of San Fruttuoso via San Rocco. The old stone-laid pavement can still be seen in places. In contrast to the more difficult coastal path followed in Walk 26, this route was suitable for laden mules — and is suitable today for the average experienced walker. Halfway along, you leave the old trail for a while, to take a detour circling round Monte di Portofino (612m), the highest summit on the peninsula. Climbing to the top isn't worth the effort: it's wooded, so there are no views. The sea views are far better from Toca, a superb picnic site, and then from the path along the mountain's southern slopes to the rock boulders of Pietre Strette. The last stretch is a long descent through typical Mediterranean pine and holm oak forest to idyllic San Fruttuoso Bay.

**Start the walk** opposite **Camogli** RAILWAY STATION: take the flight of steps down to the beginning of the coastal promenade VIA GARIBALDI. Don't follow this, but turn left and carry on along VIA BONO FERRARI, which goes past the grounds of the CENOBIO DEI DOGI luxury hotel. Behind the entrance gate take the smaller street straight ahead, running

*The mule trail between San Rocco and Gaixella*

alongside a stream. After 200m keep left; then, 30m further on, fork right on a sealed footpath (☞ SAN ROCCO, WAY-MARKS: HOLLOW RED CIRCLES AND TWO RED DOTS). This rises between old walls enclosing country houses, small gardens and olive groves. The ascending trail ends in front of **San Rocco**'s main CHURCH (220m; **45min**). The friendly little village has a splendid panoramic position on the western slopes high above the blue bay of Camogli.

Take the stepped footpath VIA GALETTI to the right of the church (☞ PORTOFINO VETTA, WAYMARKS HOLLOW RED CIRCLES). You head uphill through some houses, trailing fine sea views. Five minutes above San Rocco the route reduces to an old cobbled mule trail lined by the STATIONS OF THE CROSS depicted in naive ceramic images. Entering the wood, the trail goes past an OPEN-AIR ALTAR on the left and changes to an earthen path. Ascending the forested inland slopes of **Monte Portofino**, you come to an obvious crossing trail on the ridge, at a place signposted 'GAIXELLA' (405m; **1h25min**).

Turn right, following RED SQUARE WAYMARKS for just 100m, to a three-way fork, then take the turn-off furthest to the right (☞ PARADISO/SEMA-FORO NUOVO, RED STRIPE AND DOT WAYMARKS). The well-worn path climbs for another

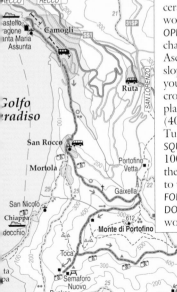

Retrace your steps to the TOCA crossing (**2h15min**) and turn right (▐ PIETRE STRETTE, STILL RED TRIANGLE WAYMARKS). The small path undulates along the steep seaside slopes of Monte Portofino. Leading through low macchia, it allows fine views down to the sea. At two places along the trail you can spot the campanile of San Fruttuoso Abbey below. Re-entering the forest, you come to a T-junction 30m below an important trail junction by the conglomerate rock boulders of PIETRE STRETTE (452m; **2h55min**).

Turn right here, to descend to San Fruttuoso (HOLLOW RED CIRCLE WAYMARKS). You are back on the old mule trail, which starts its long, steady, gradual descent to the sea. A good 15 minutes down from Pietre Strette the path emerges from the forest. After another five minutes it veers right in front of a stream (TAP for drinking water on the right), which you then cross to the left. Descending through open terrain with far-reaching sea views, you come to an ISOLATED HOUSE AND BAR in a fine position (**3h25min**); it has a shady terrace with tables and benches. Behind the building you re-enter the woods. In the shade of holm oaks you descend to the massive TORRE DORIA. Turn right at this medieval watchtower. It's only three minutes from here along a cobbled path to the entrance to SAN FRUTTOSO MONASTERY. Going through the bar of neighbouring RISTORANTE DA GIOVANNI, you arrive at the BEACH and the TWO JETTIES for the boats to Camogli or Portofino (**3h50min**).

15 minutes in a shady forest, levels out for a short while, then swings round the hillside to an ISOLATED PINK HOUSE on the left (540m). At the fork behind it, ignore the left turn uphill for 'Semaforo Vecchio'; go *downhill* towards SEMAFORO NUOVO ('new lighthouse'). Ignore a path joining from the left (waymarks change here to TWO HOLLOW RED TRIANGLES). Keep descending straight ahead on the forest trail. About 15 minutes below the pink house you come to a crossroads signposted as 'TOCA' (450m; **2h**).

Before heading left for Pietre Strette a short detour leads to a pleasant picnic spot: follow the ascending path straight on for 100m (RED TRIANGLES ); it then zigzags downhill to the right through a dark forest of holm oaks. Leaving the shade you step onto a grassy ledge with two STONE HUTS. This place is called SEMAFORO NUOVO (420m), although there is no longer any lighthouse here. A wooden table under a big pine tree makes a lovely rest area high above the blue sea.

## Walk 25: FROM SAN FRUTTUOSO TO PUNTA CHIAPPA OR CAMOGLI — STEEP CLIFFS ABOVE THE SEA

See also photograph opposite
**Distance/time:** 10km/6.2mi; 3h30min
**Grade:** strenuous, with an overall ascent/descent of 450m/1475ft. This route is not really dangerous, but you must be absolutely sure-footed and have a good head for heights; the most exposed sections are equipped with chains. Don't walk in wet weather; the stony ground becomes slippery.
**Route-finding:** easy; waymarked with double red dots throughout (*but no waymarks on the descent to Punta Chiappa*)
**Refreshments:** bars/restaurants at Punta Chiappa (fairly expensive); a bar three minutes before San Rocco (in summer only) and another in the village *alimentari* (grocer's)
**Equipment:** as pages 12-13
**Transport and Map:** see Walk 24, page 114
*Note:* In rough seas the boat does not call at Punta Chiappa!
**Alternative walks**
**1 from San Lorenzo della Costa or Santa Margherita Ligure to San Fruttuoso.** Begin by using the notes for Walk 22 or Walk 24 to get to San Fruttuoso; allow 5-6h.
**2 From Mortola to Camogli.** From the 2H45MIN-POINT in the walk, head on to the hillside village of **San Rocco** (220m; **2h50min**). Opposite the main church, turn left downhill (▪ CAMOGLI, HOLLOW CIRCLES, TWO RED DOTS). The small lane goes past a bar/grocery shop *(alimentari)* and reduces to a stepped footpath. Descending between old walls, fruit gardens, olive groves and small country houses, you quickly reach the edge of **Camogli**, where you go past the elegant HOTEL CENOBIO DEI DOGI. Keep left here, to come on to the beginning of the SEASIDE PROMENADE. Steps on the right here would take you to the RAILWAY STATION. To reach the jetty, walk ahead on VIA GARIBALDI, which runs parallel to the beach and is lined by high multicoloured façades. At the end of the beach, behind the prominent main church (SANTA MARIA ASSUNTA), you come to Camogli's small HARBOUR (**3h30min**), from where boats sail to San Fruttuoso.

T his, the most exciting walk in the Portofino Nature Reserve, is also the most demanding. The coastal path from San Fruttuoso Bay to San Rocco crosses rough, rocky terrain with some steep ups and downs. Hiking between 100 and 230 metres above the shore, you enjoy fine views to isolated bays and steep rock faces. For the first half of the walk the trail sometimes edges vertical cliffs. The second half is easy walking on good paths and small paved lanes. The hike ends by the sea, on the flat and rocky headland of Punta Chiappa. Nearby, you can pick up a boat back to Camogli or San Fruttuoso, unless the sea is too rough (in which case you'll have to climb back up to Mortola). Alternatively, skip the descent to Punta Chiappa and go directly from Mortola to Camogli (see notes for Alternative walk 2).

**Start the walk** from the jetty next to the beach: go up the steps through the bar of RISTO-RANTE DA GIOVANNI, to reach the small SQUARE in front of SAN FRUTTUOSO ABBEY. Turn left and follow the path skirting the bay, with the houses on your left (■ SAN ROCCO, WAY-MARKS; TWO RED DOTS). Some 100m from the church take the stepped footpath climbing to the right. It changes to an earthen path, which rises steeply in hairpin bends along the wooded slopes to the west of the bay. The path then swings left towards the sea, and about 20 minutes up from San Fruttuoso, you're crossing more open terrain, with the rocky coastline in view. Continuing round to the right, inland, you re-enter a shady holm oak wood. This initial climb ends on a SADDLE (245m; **40min**). From the pass the trail zigzags steeply downhill. Leaving the shade of the trees, you dip into a deserted rocky valley, where half-wild goats roam around. A short way past the lowest point in the trail you cross a stony streambed (95m; **1h05min**).

*Now the more demanding section of the walk begins. At several places you will have to clamber over rocky outcrops with the help of iron chains. With care, these*

*Between San Fruttuoso and the bunker*

*passages are mastered without big problems.*

About half an hour from the streambed you cross a slightly sloping rockface high above the sea (chains to grip). Past this, you arrive at a LEDGE with a superb panoramic view (**1h55min**). Beyond here the route becomes easier. A steady climb below steep cliffs ends at a WORLD WAR II BUNKER overlooking the **Gulf of Genoa** (230m; **2h15min**).

The rest of the route is a doddle: from the bunker the path swings right to round a rocky ledge and widens to a trail, easy underfoot. It undulates along the western slopes of the peninsula, passes a dip

with a SPRING on the right (drinking water) and ascends to the few houses of **Mortola** (220m). Cross this peaceful hamlet on the main lane. Around 200m beyond Mortola you come to a turn-off SIGNPOSTED FOR 'SAN NICOLO' (**2h45min**).

For Punta Chiappa turn left here. *(But for the Alternative walk to Camogli keep to the lane straight ahead.)* The stepped footpath *(no waymarks)* descends for 10 minutes to the small medieval church of SAN NICOLO. Turn right and pass the building, keeping it on your left. Carry on downhill on a mule trail and steps through the scattered houses of **Punta Chiappa** HAMLET. You pass the RISTORANTE MULINO DA DRIN and the TRATTORIA DO SPADIN and arrive at the seashore. Take the FOOTBRIDGE below the vertical rock face to the beginning of a flight of old stone steps. On the right here is the JETTY (**3h10min**).

To reach the headland you have to go up the steps and follow an ongoing path. Ignore the left turn signposted for 'Ristorante Stella'. You soon step onto the flat and barren, windswept land tip of **Punta Chiappa**. If the weather is calm, you could go for a swim. But there is no beach, so you have to clamber a little to get into the water. Then retrace your steps to the JETTY for your boat (**3h30min**).

# Genoa

## the changing metropolis

*Genoa, Porto Antico*

Genoa, the capital of Liguria, is a fascinating port town with many cultural sights. It's an ideal destination for a rainy day, when it's not much fun to hike. Genoa is magnificently sited, stretching east-west about 30 kilometres along a large curving bay, surrounded by the wide sheltering arc of the steep Apennines. Genoa has about 630,000 inhabitants; some 1.5 million people live in the larger metropolitan area.

The historical importance of Genoa was based on its harbour. The people here always looked across the sea to gain their wealth and power. As far back as 800 years ago people started leaving their homes in the Apennines to settle down by the coast, to find work in shipbuilding or trade. Prosperity would never be found in the unproductive soil of the hinterland. Among the coastal settlers was the family of Christopher Columbus, which moved
120

in the 15th century from the valley of Fontanabuona to Genoa.

In the Middle Ages Genoa became an independent Maritime Republic, in the 12th and 13th centuries competing for power over the Mediterranean with the similar city states of Amalfi, Venice and Pisa. With its large navy, the Republic of Genoa gained control over Corsica, Sardinia, Piedmont and the coast up to Nice. By participating in the Crusades, Genoa was able to establish trading colonies in the Middle East, the Aegean and Andalusia. After a decline in power in 14th and 15th centuries, the city's fortunes again improved in the 16th century. In 1526 Admiral Andrea Doria put the Genoese armada under the charge of the Spanish crown, thus establishing a close relationship with the leading power of its time. Genoa could profit from the Spanish exploitation of the New World, mainly as a financier, having invented the modern paperless form of financial transactions all those centuries ago. As long ago as 1407 the Banco di San Giorgio — often considered the world's first modern bank — had been founded by leading Genoese families. Genoa 'la Superba' became one of the wealthiest cities on earth.

In the 18th and 19th centuries, due to changing trade routes, Genoa's economic and political power went into steady decline. Foreign powers controlled the town. Many emigrants went to the Americas to escape poverty. But with its industrialisation after World War II, Genoa consolidated its role as a major seaport; shipyards and steelworks attracted workers from all over Italy. In 1970 the population had risen to about 800,000. The following decline of heavy industry brought high unemployment, and Genoa acquired the reputation of being a seedy big town in decay, full of criminals. But over the last two decades the town has managed to change this poor image to a large extent. It's true that there are still some shady quarters in the old town behind the harbour, as shabby as they are lively and colourful. But many places have been very successfully modernised. So Genoa attracts more and more visitors every year. Its main sights are the PORTO ANTICO with the ACQUARIO, the OLD TOWN QUARTER, the CATHEDRAL and the VIA GARIBALDI PALACES.

The PORTO ANTICO (the 'old harbour') looks very modern today. After transferring the shipping business to a new location far out to the west, it has been changed into a bustling, palm-lined promenade area by the sea, with cafes, restaurants and new tourist attractions. The well-known architect Renzo Piano, native son of Genoa, has been responsible for the design. The Acquario is Europe's largest seawater aquarium — popular with children of all ages! Nearby are the BIGO, a panoramic lift in the shape of a shipyard crane, the BOLLA, a glass sphere (tropical greenhouse), and the GALEONE NEPTUNE, a rebuilt 17th-century pirate ship. The new GALATA MUSEO DEL MARE at the northern end of the harbour takes you on a journey through the glorious history of Genoese seafaring. The PALAZZO DI SAN GIORGIO, with large 16th-century frescoes on the façade, the first seat of the Banco di San Giorgio, is the only older building remaining at the Porto Antico.

Once past the flyover (STRADA SOPRAELEVATA) you enter the old town, one of the largest in Europe. It's an intricate maze of *caruggi* — dark, narrow alleys between tall buildings, intersected by small squares and tucked-away churches. Some are lively, with small shops, food stalls, restaurants and old-fashioned cafés; some are pretty seedy, red-light areas. Old town highlights include the luxurious 16th-century PALAZZO SPINOLA, with a fine collection of mainly Flemish art— painters like Rubens, Memling, van Dyck. The gothic-style PORTA SOPRANA is one of the last remains of medieval Genoa; the little house in front of it is probably the birthplace of Columbus. The PIAZZA MATTEO, with the lovely 14th-century black- and white-striped CHIESA SAN MATTEO, was the seat of the powerful Doria family.

SAN LORENZO CATHEDRAL at the upper edge of the old town is an impressive building of medieval origin, which has undergone many changes in style over the centuries. Its zebra-striped gothic façade is decorated with rich relief work and lion figures. The interior with its black and white arches, baroque wall paintings and gold ceiling is opulent. Don't miss the treasury, with its fascinating collection of medieval religious art.

In the second half of the 16th century, wealthy Genoese bankers and traders started to move away from the confines of the old town. They built palace-like villas along the Strada Nuova ('New Street', today VIA GARI-BALDI). Walk along it and look at the inner courtyards with their rich decor — painted vaulting, classical reliefs, sculptures and columns. PALAZZA DORIA-TURSI (at number 9), connected by a gangway to PALAZZO

BIANCO (number 11), and PALAZZO ROSSO (number 18), on the opposite side of the street, make up a Museum of Fine Arts with a rich collection of Renaissance and baroque paintings from famous artists, most of them of Flemish origin.

In the 17th century the wealthy Balbi family built their seven palaces along adjoining Via Balbi, starting at the splendidly decorated CHIESA ANNUNZIATA DEL VASTATO. Probably the most splendid of all Genoese palaces is the PALAZZO REALE (number 10). It also has a fine collection of paintings. Go into the mosaic court-yard and take a look at the elegant façade at the back.

If you have enough time, there is much more to see and do. You could visit the STAGLIENO CEMETERY on the outskirts, an open-air museum of 19th-century sculp-ture, or take a boat trip on from the Acquario past the docks and quays of the modern harbour to the suburb of PEGLI, with the subtropical PALAVICINI GARDEN. Or dip into the sound, colour, smell and flavour of the MERCATO ORIENTALE, a lively old-fashioned covered market (mercato coperto) offering a large selection of local food. In the PARCO DELLA MURA, only a few kilometres from the city, are the walls and fortresses of a large 17th- to 19th-century defensive system, as well as good hiking in unspoilt nature (like Walk 27)!

## Getting about

The town has two main stations, Piazza Principe at the northern end of the inner city and Brignole to the south. Many **trains of all kinds** run from both stations along the Riviera di Levante, so all towns featuring in this book are easily reachable by train from Genoa.

Many **buses** serve the inner city. A single journey ticket, valid for 100 minutes from stamping, costs 1.50 €, a 24-hour ticket (Genovapass) 6.50 €. They are available at automats, newsstands and small shops with a black and white 'T'-sign (tabacchi). For more infor-mation and timetables see www.amt.genova.

Genoa's only **underground line** goes from Piazza Principe station via the Porto Antico to Piazza Ferrari near the cathedral.

## Walk planning

Genoa is a good place to combine holiday sightseeing and bustling city life with walking. Walks 26 and 27 start from the town itself. But all walks starting from as far south as Monterosso can be reached from Genoa as day-trips.

## Accommodation

There are countless hotels in town, most of them in the upper price range. I think the following central hotels offer good value for money: CAIROLI***, friendly small hotel near Via Garibaldi (www.hotelcairoligenova. com, 90-100 €), EUROPA***, some 100m from Piazza Principe railway station (www.hoteleuropagenova.it, 85-110 €), AGNELLO D'ORO***, next door to the Hotel Europa, but a little simpler (www.hotelagnellodoro.it, 75-105 €), SOANA**, not far from Brignole station; take a quiet room at the back (www.hotelsoana.it, 75-95 €).

## Walk 26: FROM TRASO ALTO TO RECCO — HIGH PASTURES ABOVE THE COAST

**Distance/time:** 17km/10.5mi; 5h40min

**Grade:** moderate-strenuous, with an overall ascent of 630m/2065ft and descent of 1100m/3600ft. The main challenge of this walk is its length, otherwise there are no major difficulties: with the exception of a short section around Barego, the trails and paths are in good condition, despite being quite narrow in places.

**Route-finding:** fairly easy, nearly all paths are reliably waymarked

**Equipment:** as pages 12-13

**Refreshments:** the rural bar/trattoria Case Cornua halfway along is recommended for a break, with good quality food at low prices. The menu of traditional Ligurian food changes daily (they tell you what is on offer) — so expect meals like dried stockfish or thin noodles with potato pesto rather than standard pizza or spaghetti dishes.

**Transport:** 🚌 bus from Genova to Torriglia (Mon-Sat at 8.45, departs from in front of the main exit from Brignole railway station); change at 'Traso Ponte' (the big road bridge below Traso) and take the connecting bus for Sant'Alberto, which leaves at 9.20 (immediately after the arrival of the bus from Genoa). Alight at Traso Alto at 9.30, by the main church, Sant'Ambrogio. There are more buses on workdays, with change at Bargagli via Sant'Alberto: departs Genova Brignole 8.00, Bargagli 8.40/8.45, arrives Traso Alto 9.05; departs Genova Brignole 9.50, Bargagli 10.30/10.35, arrives Traso Alto 10.55. For the return, 🚌 local train from Recco to Genova Brignole (every 30-60 minutes)

**Map:** Carta dei Sentieri, Sheet 1 Sentieri Forti di Genova, Nervi e Recco (1:25,000, FIE Federazione Italiana Escursionismo)

**Shorter walk: Colle Caprile–Sant'Apollinare–Sori.** 11km/6.8mi; 4h; moderate, with an ascent of 220m/720ft and descent of 620m/2030ft. Access by 🚌 bus from Recco to the pass of Colle Caprile above Uscio (Mon-Sat at 7.30, 8.45, 10.00, 11.15, 12.05, 12.40; Sun 8.05, 9.40, 11.10, 12,50). From the road FORK on the **Colle Caprile** (452m) walk left (southwest) towards LUMARZO, passing through **Calcinara** village. After the ALBERGO COLLE CAPRILE, turn left to the village square with its little church (**10min**). From here take VIA CHIESA uphill through the houses (WAY-MARKS: DIAGONALLY DIVIDED RED/WHITE SQUARES). This small road reduces to a path which soon crosses the GENOVA-USCIO ROAD. Continue straight ahead on a shady cobbled mule trail. Pass a small chapel and, at the fork beyond it, take a rocky path rising steeply back to the road (**25min**), then follow the road 500m uphill. Some 50m before the hillock with the CAPELLETTA DEGLI ALPINI you meet the MAIN WALK AT THE 3H-POINT (595m). Now follow the main walk to the CROSS-ROADS AT THE 4H35MIN-POINT (**2h10min**). *Leave* the main walk here, and take the path to the right (WAYMARKS: BLUE DOUBLE STRIPES ON ORANGE). At first this runs along a flat

*Sant'Ambrogio church at Traso Alto*

drops down, curves right and joins a concrete path. Follow this straight ahead past scattered houses and olive groves. Eventually you come to SANT'APOLLINARE rising on a terrace above the sea — a very attractive picture (259m; **3h20min**).

Behind the little church take a stepped path left downhill, with some houses on the right. After a left-hand bend it levels out in an olive grove. Some five minutes later, turn sharp right on a concrete walkway. Beyond a house with a PALM TREE, this reduces to an earthen mule trail heading for the coast. Joining a tarmac track, keep right, on the flat, and go past HOUSE NUMBER 17. Follow an ongoing path. At a crossroads three minutes later, turn left (WAYMARKS: TWO VERTICAL RED STRIPES). A steep flight of steps takes you down to **Sori**. From the end of the steps bear left to lovely SAN ROCCO CHURCH, with a view to Sori church and beach. Follow the path down to the main road, the VIA AURELIA (**4h**). The bus for Recco stops on the left here, some metres uphill, the bus for Genoa down to the right, on the big bridge. The side-road opposite, to the left, descends to the nearby RAILWAY STATION.

**Longer walk: Monte Croce dei Fo summit.** 35min longer than the main walk; additional ascent/descent of about 100m/325ft. From the 1H30MIN-POINT rise along the top of the grassy ridge to the left. The treeless SUMMIT (973m) is one of the best vantage points in all Liguria. On really clear days one can even spot the snow-covered high Alps.

ridge. Some 10 minutes from the crossroads it drops steeply past a CYLINDRICAL WATER TANK and becomes stony underfoot. The descent ends at the next crossroads (**2h30min**), where you turn right (RED FLASH ON A STONE, *but no further waymarks*). Follow a slightly overgrown panoramic path. At a fork 50m past a right-hand bend, keep right, uphill, at the right of some houses. Then carry on straight ahead. The path changes from concrete to earthen underfoot. After passing some more houses it narrows and descends alongside cypresses, again a little overgrown in places. Ignore a path coming up from nearby Ageno and go past an old STONE BASIN on the right (**2h45min**).

Now you contour the southeastern slopes of a ridge on a lovely path with splendid views down into Camogli Bay. After a gentle rise, the trail suddenly

T his long walk gives an impression of the contrasting aspects of the Riviera di Levante. It starts from the mountainous green hinterland behind Genoa, where you feel very far away indeed from the warmth of the Ligurian coast — although you're only a few miles away in reality. After passing through an abandoned hamlet, you climb onto pastoral grassland grazed by herds of horses and goats. Many ruins, broken drystone walls and shepherd's huts remain from the days when this landscape was the basis for a simple, poor, farming and herding culture which only disappeared gradually during last century.

From the high pastures you eventually return to the rich Mediterranean coastal scenery with its colourful hamlets and houses standing amidst sweet-scented pine forests and lovely olive groves. The entire route offers fascinating panoramic views, from the deserted Apennine mountain ranges inland to the densely populated coast around the Gulf of Genoa. For more then three hours you're traversing open ridges between the Fontanabuona Valley and the sea at a height of 500 to 900 metres.

**Start the walk** at **Traso Alto**, from the imposing church of SANT'AMBROGIO (470m). Follow the main road uphill for 50m, then turn right on a path (RED TRIANGLE WAYMARKS). It rises through a patch of wood, offering far-off views back over the clock tower of Sant'Ambrogio towards green mountains. About three minutes up from the church you meet small road (VIA ROMA). Keep right (WAYMARKS CHANGING FROM RED TRIANGLES TO RED SQUARES). The tarmac ends within five minutes, at the hamlet of **Ciappa** (510m). Go left uphill for 50m, in front of the line of houses, and turn right to pass between some RUINS. Keep left, to an old FOUNTAIN, where you again turn left on a concrete path (⏺ BAREGO). You climb to a T-junction behind HOUSE NUMBER 28A (**15min**). Turn

right (⏺ BAREGO, ANELLO DI TRASO, WAYMARKS STILL RED SQUARES).
You are now on the ancient cobbled trail to the abandoned hamlet of Barego. It gradually rises along moss-coated drystone walls in the shade of oak woods. Some five minutes uphill it joins a somewhat wider trail which soon narrows again (beyond a RUIN). This delightful old trail rises steadily, crosses a stream swings right and arrives at the scattered RUINS of **Barego** (720m; **35min**). Keep straight ahead, with the broken old walls on your left. (*Watch out, they are in danger of collapsing!*) You may find now that fallen branches hinder your progress for about 10 minutes but, once past a clearing, walking becomes easier again. Re-entering the forest, the path then crosses

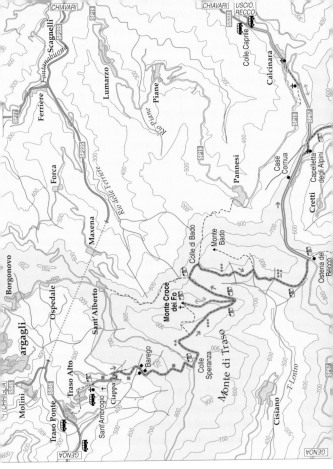

two small streams. *Watch out* for a little wooden SIGN, warning that the trail ahead will turn sharp left. Soon after, the trail enters open grassland, running along the northern slopes of **Monte Traso** (883m). It veers right in front of a ditch and leads uphill onto the saddle of **Colle Speranza**, where the sea becomes visible (835m; **1h**).

Cross the tarmac road on the saddle and turn left on a grassy trail gently rising on the south side of a HILLOCK WITH A CROSS on top. Some five minutes from Colle Speranza the trail swings left downhill. You go through a GATE and keep

straight ahead across the meadows to a METAL HUT on a saddle southwest of **Monte Croce dei Fo** (815m; **1h10min**). Turn right here and take a grassy trail running along the southern slopes of the mountain (WAYMARKS THREE RED DOTS, ALSO SINGLE RED DOT AND TRIANGLE). At a fork past another gate, take the lower path (WAYMARKS NOW JUST THREE RED DOTS). It contours along the open slopes. You may encounter herds of goats or half-wild horses up here. A short ascent takes you onto a ledge (882m; **1h30min**). From here a diversion to the SUMMIT OF MONTE

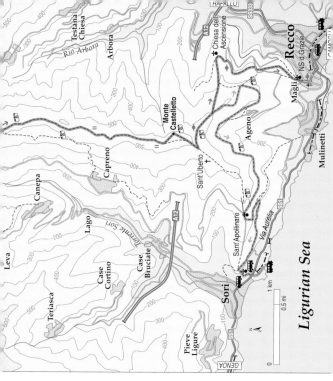

CROCE DEI FO is possible (Longer walk).

Crossing the ledge, the path bears round to the left and descends along the eastern slopes of the mountain. It emerges on **Colle di Bado**, the grassy saddle between Monte Croce dei Fo and Monte Bado (760m; **1h45min**). From the eastern end of the saddle a lovely path descends gently, keeping constantly to the western slopes of **Monte Bado** (WAYMARKS STILL THREE RED DOTS). At a fork some 15 minutes down from Colle di Bado, keep right and cross a rocky streambed. Ignore a trail rising to the left, to the Monte Bado summit (**2h10min**), and carry straight on, slightly downhill (WAYMARKS NOW THREE RED DOTS, PLUS SINGLE RED DOT AND STRIPE). The path gradually swings round to the left, into a side-valley, where it

bears right and leads through a thin forest of oaks. Circling to the left, it passes broken drystone walls and old STONE HUTS. At the decayed buildings of the OSTERIA DEL BECCO it joins the GENOVA–USCIO ROAD (721m; **2h35min**).

Follow this downhill along the panoramic seaside slopes. A good 15 minutes down from Osteria del Becco you pass the bar/trattoria CASE CORNUA on the left. Keep to the road for another five minutes, then take a short detour: a small path to the right takes you onto the viewpoint-hillock with the CAPELLETTA DEGLI ALPINI. From the small chapel, go downhill, back to the road. After about 50m, your ongoing path to Recco leaves the road to the right (595m; **3h**). *(The shorter walk starting from Colle Caprile joins here.)*

The lovely path (▪ S APOLLI-

NARE, RED PARALLEL STRIPE WAYMARKS) descends over old terraces along the open hillside. After entering a forest, ignore a first path forking off left for Testana, and 30m ahead a second one off down to the right for Capreno. Your path, signposted for S. Apollinare, always keeps to the long range of hills descending gradually towards the sea. Initially it runs along the western slopes. Then it leads alongside drystone walls across the ridge to the eastern side, which is soon left again by a short steep climb to the right. The path crosses small patches of wood and grassy clearings. You pass a hillock on the left with a small PYLON. Crossing some meadows, you find yourself once more on the MIDDLE OF THE RIDGE (**3h30min**).

At the fork three minutes later, keep right. The path again runs along the western slopes, a little below the top of the ridge. Down in the valley you can see the clock tower at Canepa. For some 50m you walk on the ridge, then keep a little to the right. The trail leads through shady oak woods and past old walls and RUINS, the remains of a once-intensive pastoral life. Gradually the forest thins out and the vegetation changes to more Mediterranean species. Go past a meadow with a large RUIN on the right. At the fork at its far end, take the path to the left. It leads uphill past a PYLON onto flat **Monte Castelletto** (565m), where you enjoy splendid views into Camogli Bay. From the summit the stony path drops down for five minutes. When it levels out, about 250m before SANT' UBERTO, a huge STELE with a statue of Christ visible from far off, fork sharp left (493m; **4h20min**).

The panoramic path (⊪ RECCO, RED WAYMARKS: CIRCLE DIVIDED BY A STRIPE) descends gently, swinging right along the hillside thinly covered with pines, holm oaks and strawberry trees. At the edge of a thicker forest you reach a CROSSROADS (395m; **4h35min**). Ignore a blue- and orange-waymarked path off to the right; keep ahead. *(But for the Shorter walk turn right here.)* You soon arrive at the little CHIESA DELL'ASCENSIONE (262m; **4h50min**). The path curves to the right here and descends past some houses to a small road, VIA FAVETO. *Leave* the waymarked route here and keep right. The road rapidly ends. Continue straight ahead on an old path, via some terraced gardens. About 10 minutes later the path rejoins VIA FAVETO. Follow this 50m to the right, then take a footpath off left. You walk through olive groves and past some houses, then descend a flight of steps, leading to the large baroque church NOSTRA SIGNORA DELLE GRAZIE in **Megli** (115m; **5h20min**).

Cross the road below the church and continue straight ahead on SALITA PER MEGLI. At a SHRINE on the right, turn left. Descend along the stepped SALITA PER MEGLI. Cross a first road and then the main road (the VIA AURELIA), to meet the small VIA ROMANA. Follow this to the left, cross the VIA AURELIA once more, and enter **Recco** (**5h40min**). The main BUS STOP is under the big railway bridge; the RAILWAY STATION a short way uphill to the right of the rail lines.

## Walk 27: FROM GRANAROLO TO CAMPI VIA THE PARCO DELLA MURA — THE FORTRESSES OF GENOA

**Distance/time:** 10km/6.2mi; 3h45min
**Grade:** easy-moderate, with an overall ascent of 610m/2000ft and descent of 430m/1410ft
**Route-finding:** many forks and few waymarks up to the 1h35min-point — so you have to pay close attention; easy for the rest of the walk
**Equipment:** as pages 12-13
**Refreshments:** bar-pizzeria at Colle di Trensasco (closed Mon/Tue); small bar at Campi train stop (seasonal opening)
**Transport:** 🚋 Granarolo rack railway (leaves about every 40 minutes from the small stop next to a bar some 5 minutes' walking to the west of Piazza Principe railway station. Return on 🚋 narrow gauge railcar from Campi to Genoa Piazza Manin (Mon-Fri at 12.42, 14.20, 15.30, 16.55, 18.02, 19.06, 19.57; Sat at 14.20, 15.30, 17.03, 18.10, 19.37; Sun at 12.50, 15.26, 17.05, 18.46); timetables see www.ferroviagenovacasella.it. Then 🚌 city bus 34 from Piazza Manin to Piazza Principe railway station (frequent)
**Map:** as Walk 26, page 125

In many respects Genoa is an unusual Italian metropolis. It extends over thirty kilometres along the coast from east to west, but only stretches inland for two to three kilometres at some points. So in some places there is hardly any transition from the tightly packed houses of the inner city and the virtually uninhabited grassy ridges of the Apennines. This means that a quick escape from the busy town centre into open countryside is always possible. And the little nature reserve, the Parco della Mura to the north of Genoa's old harbour, offers ample good hiking opportunities.

On this walk across grassy panoramic heights you encounter the gloomy ruins of four fortresses. In the troubled 14th century, the Genoese started building protective walls and forts on the surrounding hillsides. By the 18th and 19th centuries, this network had developed into one of the biggest defense systems in Europe. More than 10 fortresses and a rampart wall 13 kilometres long safeguarded the wealthy town. Luckily they never had to prove their suitability.

Everyone — not just train buffs — will enjoy getting to and returning from this walk. We take a rack railway up to Granarolo and return from Campi on the little 'Trenino', one of Italy's last narrow gauge railways.

**Start the walk** from the terminus of **Granarolo** RACK RAILWAY (210m). Walk uphill on the pedestrianised lane, SALITA DI GRANAROLO, passing through Granarolo village. Keep ahead and go past the right turn for the CHURCH. At

the following fork turn right to climb between old walls and join a small tarmac road. Follow this some 50m uphill through a right-hand bend, then take a paved footpath rising to the left. Beyond some houses this reduces to a mule trail leading back to the road. Follow this past a tall *RED/ WHITE TRANSMITTER* on the right. A good 200m past the mast, turn right on a path running along an open grassy slope (**20min**, *RED CIRCLE WAYMARKS*).

After crossing another trail, the path descends steeply for 30m, then levels off by swinging left.

Ahead you look into empty green hills, behind down on the old harbour and the abruptly ending sea of houses that make up Genoa. The old mule trail enters a stand of wood with pines and holm oaks and curves right to cross a small stream. From here it rises steeply for three minutes, to a small road. Follow this to the left, past *TRATTORIA POLVERIERA* on the left, to join a somewhat wider road. A rough old *STONE BUILDING* at the left was once a storage room for gunpowder (*polveriera*). On the following right-hand bend, leave the tarmac by heading left on a woodland trail rising to the west *(no waymarks)*. About five minutes from the road it bends right and climbs the wooded slope to a TARMAC TRACK (**1h**). Follow this popular jogging route, circling to the right, until you meet another road. Cross this to the left, to step into a grassy square at the eastern edge of the huge 17th-century Genoese defensive wall, the MURA NUOVE (**1h10min**). From the balustrade you look across the Bisagno Valley onto flat fortresses.

Follow the wall inland, turn right, and then immediately left on a side-road. It rises along the inside of the Mura Nuove towards Forte Sperone towering above. About 100m before a old ROUND WATER TANK (SERBATOIO), fork right on an earthen path. It rises through a small oak wood, to a small road in front of FORTE SPERONE (500m; **1h25min**). This 17th-century fortress, standing at the far northern point of the Mura Nuove, played a key role in the Genoese defence system. It has a moat with a drawbridge. The entrance gate is decorated with the heraldic lion of the Dukes of Savoy. Unfortunately, the interior is closed to the public because it's in such a bad state of repair. From the balustrade at the west you have far-off views across the Polcevera Valley. Steps lead from here down to the entrance to a dark tunnel passageway.

From the fortress walk down the access road for five minutes, to where the tunnel passage exits. (If you have a torch, you could use the tunnel itself.) Keep right here and follow a path along MURA NUOVE. Where it rejoins the road, veer right, through the gate of FORTE BEGATO (**1h35min**). Turn right again, on the earthen trail rising with the enclosure of Forte Sperone on your right (RED CIRCLE WAYMARKS). At the upper end of the Forte Sperone compound, a path off to the right allows a short diversion to the MOAT at the sharply north side of the fortress. Your ongoing route keeps to the grassy open ridge, heading for the next fortress, already visible. It is reached by a smaller path *(no waymarks)* forking right from the main trail (597m; **1h50min**). Small, square FORTE PUIN was only built between 1815 and 1831 as a first defensive outpost to the north of the Mura Nuove.

At the foot of the steps up to the fortress entrance, take a path off right; this curves to the east of the building through heather. Some 10 minutes from Forte Puin, the path swings left and crosses the main trail on the ridge. Keep ahead on a panoramic path going uphill along the seaward southern slopes. It ends in front of FORTE FRATELLO MINORE (622m; **2h10min**). This 'Little Brother's Fort' was erected between 1747 and 1832. Together with the Forte Fratello Maggiore ('Big Brother's Fort') — no longer in existence — it safeguarded the northwestern flank of the Genoese defensive system.

Some 50m in front of Forte Fratello Minore turn sharp right and climb onto the flat hillock to the east, the former site of Forte Fratello Maggiore. A steep path drops from here

*Forte Diamante*

to the **Colle del Diamante** (565m; **2h25min**) at the foot of a big fortress visible from far off. From this saddle a cobbled military trail zigzags uphill to **Forte Diamante** (667m; **2h 40min**). This fort was built in 1758 on the summit of a steep, isolated, barren hill. It is the northernmost Genoese bulwark. Its excellent strategic position is unmistakable: from up here the views reach from the sea far inland to the valleys and mountain ranges of the Apennines.

There is a direct path from Forte Diamante downhill to the Colle di Trensasco, but it is uncomfortable. So it's best to retrace your steps to the **Colle del Diamante**. Leave your outward route here and take a small path half-left (ꞁ *PASSO GIANDINO, WHITE DOUBLE STRIPE WAYMARKS ON RED*). It descends diagonally along the eastern slope. At a notch in the hillside, the **Passo Giandino**

134

(**3h10min**), you meet an obvious crossing trail. This is the VIA DEL SALE, the ancient stone-laid SALT TRAIL from Genoa harbour to the mountainous hinterland. Follow this to the left (RED 'X' WAYMARKS). Beyond a small wood you join a somewhat wider trail. Keep straight on. The flat trail, easy underfoot, contours along the eastern hillside. In early summer masses of yellow-blooming broom line the trail. After passing the simple bar/pizzeria BAITA DEL DIAMANTE you arrive at the pass of **Colle di Trensasco** (392m), where the small GENOA–SANT'OLCESE ROAD crosses.

Follow the road 30m to the right, then take an earthen woodland track forking left *(no waymarks)*. Some five minutes from Colle di Trensasco a little wooden sign alerts you to a small path off left. It takes you to the nearby **Campi** TRAIN STOP (**3h45min**).

# Index

Geographical entries only are included here; for other entries, see Contents, page 3. A page number in **bold type** indicates a photograph; a page number in *italics* a map; both may be in addition to a text reference on the same page.